# Father of Faith Missions

by

J. Hudson Taylor

AUTOBIOGRAPHY OF J. HUDSON TAYLOR
IN SPECIAL ENGLISH

Gospel Publishing Mission

P.O. Box 1065 ~ Hobe Sound, FL 33475
www.gospelpublishingmission.org
A ministry of Hope International Missions

Translated from the original text into Special English by:
Joseph E. Taylor, *Editor-in-chief*
Terry Pollard, *Editor/Translator*
with assistance from: Juanita G. Taylor.

---

For information about other Special English books visit our web site at:
**www.gospelpublishingmission.org**

First Printing 1995
Second Printing 1998
Third Printing 1999
Fourth Printing 2000
Fifth Printing 2001
Sixth Printing 2005

Father of Faith Missions
IN SPECIAL ENGLISH



ISBN 0-9618730-0-0

This edition published in Special English by Gospel Publishing Mission by arrangement with Bethany House Publishers. Originally published under the title A Retrospect; later published under the title To China With Love. Unless otherwise indicated, Scripture references are the publishers own paraphrase.

# Table of Contents

## Important Note

Special English is a very easy-to-read vocabulary of about 1,500 basic English words. This is especially helpful to young readers and for those who speak English as a second language.

There are times when it is necessary to use words which are not in the group of words that makes up Special English. The meaning of these words is given at the end of that chapter or in the glossary at the back of the book. The first time these words are used they have a special marking like this: oatmeal[G]. When you see a word marked with a "G" like this, look in the glossary for the meaning.

CHAPTER ONE

# The Power of Prayer

This is the story of some of the happenings which led to the beginning of the China Inland Mission. The story first appeared in the pages of *China's Millions*, the monthly magazine of C.I.M. which has been published since 1875. Many readers asked that it be made into a separate book. Miss Guinness included it in the Story of the China Inland Mission, outlining the story of God's goodness to C.I.M. until the beginning of 1894. Because friends still wanted it in a separate small book, this new book has been published. Much of the material was taken from messages given in China during a meeting of our missionaries.

It is always helpful to us to fix our thinking on the spiritual side of Christian work and to understand that the work of God does not mean so much man's work for God, as God's own work through man. In our special place of being workers together with Him, we see all the help and blessings given to a sinful world through the message of the Gospel. Yet, we should never lose sight of the higher part of our work - that of obeying God and bringing honour to His name.

In so doing, we make the heart of our God and Father happy by living and serving as His children. Many things to do with my own early life and service showed this part of our work clearly to me. As I recall some of the good people I have met, I think of how much is owed to those who never have been able to see the mission field. Many are not able to give large amounts of their material things. Yet they will be greatly surprised in the Great Day to see how much work has been done by their love, their sympathy and their prayers.

For me and for the work that I have been permitted to do for God, I am very thankful to my mother and father whom I love and honour. They have passed away and entered into rest, but the influence of their lives will remain.

In about 1830, my father had read several books and was deeply troubled about the spiritual condition of China. He was especially moved by the travels of Captain[G] Basil Hall. My father was a serious and effective evangelist at home but his own situation did not allow him ever to go to China. However, he was led to pray that if God should give him a son, he would be called and honoured to labour in that large needy nation which was then so closed to the Gospel.

I did not learn of this prayer until my return to England, more than seven years after I had sailed for China. It was very interesting to find out how this early prayer had been answered.

As I grew, I found myself to be in poor health. For many years, my mother and father had lost all hope of my becoming a missionary in China. When the time came, God gave me good health and protected my life. I was given strength for much hard service both in the mission field and at home. This helped me overcome where many stronger men and women have failed.

I had many chances in early years to learn the true value both of prayer and the Word of God. It gave great happiness to my parents to teach me that if there truly was a God, it was important for us to trust Him, obey Him, and be fully given to His service. Yet, even with my spiritual background, my heart was still unchanged. Often, I had tried to make myself a Christian but failed in my efforts. I began to think that for some reason, I could not be saved. The best I could do was to enjoy the things of this world now, as there was no hope of heaven for me after I died.

I met some people who said they did not believe in God or the Bible and I accepted their ideas. I was very thankful for some hope of escape from the ruin which was waiting for those who would not repent of their sins. It may seem unusual to say this, but I have often felt thankful for the experience of this time with unbelievers. These friends used to criticise people who claimed both to be Christians and to believe their Bibles, yet did not live by their Christian faith.

I often expressed the idea that if I claimed to believe the Bible, I would try at any cost to put it to a fair test. If it failed to prove true and faithful, I would throw it out completely. I held these thoughts when the Lord was pleased to bring me to Himself. I can truthfully say that since then, I have put God's Word to the test. Certainly it has never failed me. I have never had reason to be sorry for the trust I have placed in its promises nor for following the directions I have found in the Bible.

My mother and beloved sister prayed for my salvation. Let me tell you how God answered their prayers. I was about fifteen years of age. On a day which I shall never forget, my mother was away from home, giving me the chance to have a holiday. In the afternoon, I looked through my father's collection of books to find something to read in my free hours. Nothing looked interesting so I turned over a box of small books, and chose a Gospel story which looked interesting, saying to myself, "There will be a story at the beginning, and a Gospel message at the close. I will take the first and leave the last for those who like it."

I sat down to read the little book, completely careless about the Gospel message. I believed that if there were salvation it was not for me. I planned to put away the story as soon as it became uninteresting. I should say that it was common in those days to call being born again "becoming serious." By looking at the faces of some who said they were born again, it appeared to be a very serious thing. It would be well if the people of God always had "newborn" faces, giving evidence of the blessings and happiness of salvation. If they clearly looked saved, the unsaved people would have to call their condition "becoming happy" instead of "becoming serious."

Little did I know at the time what was going on in the heart of my mother, one hundred kilometres away. She got up from eating dinner that afternoon with a strong hope for the salvation of her boy. Being away from home and having free time, she had a special chance to pray for me.

Going to her room and locking the door, she decided to stay there until her prayers were answered. Hour after hour, my mother prayed for me until at last she could pray no longer. All she could do was to praise God for showing, through His Spirit what had already been done - the salvation of her only son.

At that same time I had taken up this little story book. I was hit with this one sentence, "The *finished* work of Christ." I wondered about why the writer had used the word. Why did he not talk of the atoning work of Christ? Immediately the words "It is finished" came to my mind. What was finished? I quickly answered, "A full and perfect atonement for sin, that which I owed was paid by Jesus who took my punishment. Christ died for my sins and not for mine only, but also for the sins of the whole world."

Then came this thought, "If the whole work was finished and all that I owed was paid, what is there left for me to do?" With this, began the happy conviction, as light from the Holy Spirit shone into my soul, that there was nothing in the world to do but to fall down on my knees and accept this Saviour and His salvation, praising Him forever. So, while my mother was praising God on her knees in her room, I was praising Him in the old storehouse to which I had gone to read the little book alone.

Several days passed before I told my sister of this new found happiness. Even then, it was only after she had promised not to tell anyone of my soul secret. When our mother came home two weeks later, I was the first to meet her at the door and tell her I had such good news to give.

I can almost feel my mother's arms around my neck, as she held me and said, "I know, my boy; I have been praising the Lord for two weeks because of the good news you have to tell me." I asked in surprise, "Why, has Amelia broken her promise? She said she would tell no one." My mother told me that it was not from any human that she had learned the news and went on to tell me of her experience. You will agree with me that it would be very unusual if I were not a believer in the power of prayer.

That was not all. A short time later, I found a diary[G] exactly like my own. I opened the pages to find that it belonged to my sister. At the place it opened, she had written that she would give herself daily to prayer until God answered with the salvation of her brother. One month later, the Lord was pleased to turn me from darkness to light.

I grew up and was saved in a circle of loving family and friends. From the beginning of my Christian life, I was led to feel that God's promises were very real. I was made to understand that prayer was a very serious matter of doing business with God, for one's self or for others for whom we pray.

CHAPTER TWO

# The Call to Service

After a time, the first happy feeling of being born again passed away. This was followed by a painful dead feeling in my soul and considerable personal conflict. But this also came to an end, leaving a deeper understanding of personal weakness and dependence on the Lord as the only Keeper and Saviour of His people. The calm rest of trusting in our kind Heavenly Father is so sweet to the soul that is tired and disappointed in its fight against sin.

Not many months after being born again, I had a free afternoon and went to my own room to spend it in prayer with God. Well do I remember that time. With a happy heart, I poured out my soul before God. Again and again I told Him of my thankful love to Him who had done everything for me. He had saved me when I had given up all hope and desire for salvation. I asked Him to give me some work to do for Him, so that I could show my love and thankfulness. I needed some self-denying service, whatever it might be, however difficult or however unimportant.

He had done so much for me. I wanted to do something for Him with which He would be pleased. Having completely given myself to Him, I had put myself, my life, my friends, my all, on the altar. A deep seriousness came over my soul with the understanding that my offering was accepted. God came to my heart in a very powerful way and I was only fifteen years old. I remember being there quietly before Him. His greatness was beyond my understanding and my heart filled with happiness.

For what service I was accepted, I did not know. Yet, a deep understanding came to me that I was no longer my own. This conviction has never weakened and has controlled my everyday life. Two or three years later, an unusually good offer was made for me to study medicine. The condition was that I work for a number of years for the doctor who was my friend. But I felt I should not accept any agreement like this, being not my own to give myself away. I did not know when or how He might call for service. I belonged to Him alone and felt the responsibility always to keep myself free to obey His call.

Only a few months after this, the understanding came into my soul that the Lord wanted me to serve Him in China. It seemed that the work to which I was called was almost sure to cost my life. China was not open then as it is now. Very few missions had workers in China and there were very few books about bringing the Gospel to the people of this country.

I was happy to find that a pastor in my home town was able to lend me a copy of the book *China*, written by Medhurst. He asked me why I wanted to read it. I told him that God had called me to spend my life in missionary service in that land. He asked about how I planned to go there. I said that I did not know, but it seemed that I should do as the Twelve and the Seventy had done in Judea and go without purse[1] or scrip,[2] trusting in God to provide all my needs.

Kindly putting his hand on my shoulder, the minister answered, "Ah, my boy, as you get older you will get wiser than that. This idea did very well in the days when Christ Himself was on earth, but not now."

I have grown older since then, but not wiser. I believe more than ever that we should take as our guide, the directions of our Master and the promises He gave to His first disciples. We will find them to be just as true now as when the words were first spoken. Medhurst's book on China placed much value on medical work by missionaries which directed my thinking that skill in medicine would be a valuable tool to help spread the Gospel.

My parents gave me no direction in my decision to become a missionary. They told me that if mission work was my desire, I should use all the ways in my power to strengthen my body, mind, heart, and soul. I should wait prayerfully on God. They advised that if He showed that I was mistaken, I should be willing to follow His directions. On the other hand, I should be ready to go forward if He opened the way to missionary service.

Since that time, I have often found this advice to be very true. I began training outdoors to strengthen my body. I stopped sleeping on my soft bed and tried to do away with many extra things that made life easy. I was preparing for a rougher life. As well, I made use of any chance to pass out Gospel tracts, teach Sunday school and visit the poor and sick.

After a time of study at home, I went to Hull to begin medical training and became assistant to a doctor who worked with the school of medicine. He was also a doctor to a number of factories. Injured workers often came to our office, giving me the chance to see and carry out simple methods of surgery.

Here something happened that I must tell about. Before leaving home, I thought of paying tithe from my pay or other income. I considered it wise to study the question with my Bible in hand before I went away from home. I was concerned that I might later find myself in a difficult situation which would effect my thinking and cause me to make a mistake.

I decided to give, for the Lord's service, not less than one-tenth of whatever money I earned or came to me. With the pay I received as medical helper in Hull, I would have been able fulfil my plan very easily. Because of changes in the family of my friend and employer, I had to find another place to live. A good place to stay was found with a family member. I was thankful that my pay included the amount to be paid for my room and food.

The question now came to mind, should I or not, tithe the amount I paid for room and food. This was a part of my pay. If it had been a question of government income tax, I would certainly have to pay. On the other hand, to take a tithe from the whole amount would not leave me enough for other needs. For a short time, I was very ashamed and did not know what to do.

After much thought and prayer, I left this nice place and happy circle of family and found a small room near the edge of town. There was a sitting room and bedroom in one. I bought my own food instead of being fed by the owner of the house. In this way, I was able to tithe all of my income. I felt the change because it made me lonely and was not as nice. Yet, the Lord gave me much happiness for following His Word.

My new situation allowed more time than would have been possible before to study the Bible, visit the poor, preach and witness. Meeting many people who were in need, I soon saw that it was good to find ways to spend even less. Soon, I did not find it difficult to give away much more than the tithe of my pay on which I had at first decided.

About this time, a friend called my thinking to the question of the Second Coming of our Lord Jesus Christ. Without comment, he gave me a list of Scriptures about it and asked me to think about the matter. I gave much time to this study and was led to see that Jesus rose from the dead and was to come again. His feet would one day stand on the Mount of Olives (Zech. 14:4) and He would take the seat of government of his father David that was promised before His birth.

I saw that through all the New Testament, the coming of the Lord was the great hope of His people. This hope was always held as the strongest reason for giving ourselves in service to God. The promise of His return brings great ease to our hearts and minds in times of trouble. I also learned that the time of His return was not shown. Our responsibility is to live from day to day and from hour to hour, as men who wait for the Lord to return. Living like this, there is no worry about when He may come. The important thing is to be so ready for His coming that we are able, at any time, to give a report of our lives with a heart full of happiness and not be ashamed.

The effect of this happy and great hope was a completely useful one. It led me to look carefully through my little collection of books to see if there were any that I no longer needed. In the same way, I examined my small collection of clothes to be very sure that I owned nothing that I would be sorry to have if the Master came at once. The result was that the collection of books became much smaller than before. I gave them to help some poor people who lived nearby. For it, I received a great spiritual gain and happiness in my own soul. I also found I had some clothing which others needed more than I did.

It has been very helpful for me to do this again and again. I have never looked through my house, from top to bottom, without receiving a great spiritual blessing. I believe we are all in danger of collecting things which would be useful to others, that we do not need. It may simply be the result of carelessness. Keeping these things causes us a loss of spiritual joy.

If all the materials of the Church of God were wisely used, how much more might be done for the Lord's work! How many poor might be fed and the naked clothed? How many of those might hear who have not yet heard the Gospel? Let me advise that we all look at our things in this way very often. This will be of great spiritual value when we are able to give our extra things away.

[1] Purse: a bag for money.
[2] Scrip: a bag for food.

CHAPTER THREE

# Preparing for Service

I now had two things in mind. I needed to learn to live in difficult conditions and to live on less money. This would make me better able to help those among whom I lived and worked to bring the Gospel. I soon found that I could live on much less than I had first thought possible. By eating mainly oatmeal[1] and rice, I found that a very small amount of money was enough for my needs.

In this way, I had more than two-thirds of my pay free for other uses. What I found was that the less I spent on myself and the more I gave away, the more my happiness grew. My heart was filled with happiness beyond my understanding, all the day, and every day. It was an honour to serve my real, living God in this way.

For me, it was a very serious thing to think of going out to China, far away from all human help. There I had no choice but to depend on the loving God alone for protection, food and help of every kind. I felt that my spiritual being needed to be strengthened for such a task. I always reminded myself that if faith did not fail, God would not fail.

But then, what if one's faith should prove to be too weak? I had not at that time learned that even *"if we are faithless, he will remain faithful, for He cannot deny Himself."* (2 Timothy 2:13) I held a very serious question in my mind. The matter was not of Him being faithful or not. I questioned that my faith was strong enough to allow me to enter into this great work set before me.

I thought that when I got out to China, I should have no claim on anyone for anything. My only claim would be on God. Because of this, it became very important to learn, before leaving England to move man, through God, by prayer alone!"

At Hull, my kind employer asked me to remind him whenever my pay became due because he was always very busy. This I decided not to do directly, but to ask God to cause him to remember. In this way, my faith would be strengthened by answered prayer.

At one time, the day came near to be paid for three month's work. As usual, I was praying much about it. The time came, but my friend said nothing. I continued praying and days passed on, but he did not remember. At last, one Saturday night, I found myself with only one coin, one half crown.[2] Still, I had all I needed and continued praying.

That Sunday was a very happy one. As usual, my heart was full and overflowing with blessing. After the church service in the morning, my afternoons and evenings were filled with Gospel work in the lodging houses[G] in the poorest part of the town. I was so happy. At times it almost seemed as if Heaven had begun in my heart. All that I could want was a larger heart to hold more happiness.

After finishing my last service about ten o'clock that night, a poor man asked me to go and pray with his dying wife. I quickly agreed. On the way to his house I asked him why he had not sent for the priest, as the sound of his voice told me he was from Ireland. He advised that he had done that but the priest refused to come without being paid eighteen pence. The man's family was starving and he had no money. At this very time, I remembered that all the money I had in the world was the half crown coin. I had a bowl of soup at home for supper. There was enough food in the house for breakfast in the morning, but nothing for dinner tomorrow.

At once, there was no happiness in my heart. Instead of admitting my own lack of faith and refusal to obey, I began to tell the poor man that he was very wrong to have allowed things to get into such a condition. He should have asked the government officer for help. He said he had done this and was told to come at eleven o'clock the next morning, but he was afraid that his wife might not live through the night.

"Ah," I thought, "if only I had two shillings[G] and a sixpence[G] instead of this half crown[G], how happy I would be to give these poor people one shilling of it!" But to part with the half crown was far from my thoughts. It did not come to my mind that the real truth was simply that I could trust in God and one-and-sixpence. However, I was not yet prepared to trust Him only, without any money in my pocket.

The poor man led me into a court and I followed with some fear. I had gone there before and had been given some rough treatment. My tracts were torn to pieces and I was warned not to come again. I felt more than a little concerned. Still, it was the path of duty and I followed on. He led me up to the second floor and into a very poor room.

What a terrible sight! Four of the five poor children stood about, their thin faces telling clearly the story of slow starvation. On a blanket on the floor was a poor mother, almost dead, holding a very small, newly born child, thirty-six hours old. The child was not able to cry but only made a sad noise, for it too seemed too weak and failing. Again I thought, "if I had two shillings and a sixpence instead of half a crown, how happy I would be to give them one-and-sixpence of it!" But still a terrible unbelief stopped me from obeying the calling in my heart to help them at the cost of all I had.

It will not seem unusual that I was unable to give hope to these poor people. I needed that myself. I began to tell them that they must not lose hope, that even if they were in great trouble, there was a kind and loving Father in Heaven. But something told me that I was acting a lie by telling these unsaved people about a kind and loving Father in Heaven, and not being prepared to trust Him without half a crown!" I could hardly get my breath. How easily I would have compromised with my conscience if I had had a florin and a sixpence! I would have given the florin thankfully and kept the rest. But I was not yet prepared to trust in God alone, without the sixpence.

Under these conditions, talking was impossible. Yet, I thought I should have no difficulty in praying. This was a happy thing to me in those days. Time spent in prayer never seemed to make me tired. It was easy to find words as I prayed. I seemed to think that I would only have to kneel and start praying and that help would come to them and to me.

"You asked me to come and pray with your wife," I said to the man, "let us pray." And I knelt down. But I had just opened my mouth to say "Our Father who art in heaven," when my conscience said, "Will you make light of God? Will you kneel down and call Him Father with that half crown in your pocket?" Such a time of conflict came upon me as I have never felt before or since. How I got through that prayer I do not know. I cannot recall if the words I spoke were connected but I was very troubled as I got up from my knees.

The poor father turned to me and said, *"You see what a terrible condition we are in. If you can help us, in God's name, do!"* Just then the words quickly came into my mind, *"Give to the one who asks you,"* (Matthew 5:42) and in the word of a King there is power. (Ecclesiastes 8:4) I put my hand into my pocket, slowly took out the half crown, and gave it to the man. I told him that it might seem a small thing for me to help them, seeing that I was not in such a bad condition as they. Yet, in parting with that coin, I was giving my all.

What I had been trying to tell him was very true - God really was a Father and might be trusted. The happiness came back in a full flood to my heart. I knew in my heart that God was pleased with me. That which stopped my spiritual happiness was gone. I hoped that it was gone forever.

Not only was the poor woman's life saved, but I saw that my life was saved too! My Christian life and faith would have been a wreck if I had not obeyed the faithful leading of God's Spirit. I found the grace of God to be stronger than all my problems.

I remember that night very well. As I went home, my heart was as light as my pocket. The empty streets were filled with a song of praise which I could not hold back. I thought as I ate my bowl of soup before going to bed that I would not have exchanged it for a great feast. When I knelt to pray at my bedside, I reminded the Lord of His own Word, that he who gives to the poor lends to the Lord. I asked Him not to let me lend it for long, or I would have no dinner the next day. Having peace within and peace without, I spent a happy, restful night.

The next morning, the mailman was at the door before I finished eating my breakfast. I did not usually receive letters on Monday because my family and friends did not mail letters on Saturday. And so, I was somewhat surprised when my landlady came in, holding a large letter. I looked at the letter, but could not make out the handwriting. It was not one that I could remember and the other markings were not clear.

Where it came from I could not tell. On opening the letter, I found nothing written but some fine gloves inside a piece of paper. To my great surprise, half a sovereign fell to the ground. “Praise the Lord!” I said quickly; “400 percent for twelve hours’ use. That is a good rate of interest. How happy the business men of Hull would be if they could lend their money at such a rate!” I decided then that the Bank of Heaven which could not break should have all of my money. This is something I have never been sorry for.

I cannot tell you how often my mind has returned to this incident. Since that time, it has been such a help to me in difficult times. If we are faithful to God in little things, we will gain training and strength that will help us in the more serious trials of life.

[1] Oatmeal: a grain food.

[2] Explanation of English money that is used in this book:

- [a] Pence or Penny = coin of smallest value.
- [b] Shilling = 12 Pence.
- [c] Florin = 2 Shillings.
- [d] Half Crown = 2.5 Shillings.
- [e] Crown = 5 Shillings.
- [f] Pound or Sovereign = 20 Shillings.

[3] Lodging house: a very low class hotel.

CHAPTER FOUR

# More Answers to Prayer

This unusual and merciful help from God was a great blessing to me, adding much strength to my faith. But ten shillings, however carefully used, will not go very far. It was necessary to continue in prayer, asking that my employer remember the larger part of my pay which I had not yet received. All my prayers seemed to be unanswered. Before two weeks had passed, I had the same difficulty as experienced on that Sunday night that I remembered so well.

I became more serious in asking God to remind my employer that the pay was late. It was not the need of money that troubled me. I could have had that at any time by just asking. But the big question in my mind was if I could go to China or not. I was troubled that my lack of faith and power with God would prove to be so serious as to stop me from entering this great and honorable work.

As the week ended, I felt very ashamed. There was not only me to think of. On Saturday night, a payment was due to the Christian woman whose room I rented. I knew she needed it for her own living. I was troubled with the question of asking for my pay, so that I could give her the money I owed. Yet, by doing that, I would admit to myself that I was not able to do the work of a missionary.

When I had free time from work, I gave nearly all of Thursday and Friday to serious calling on God in prayer. But still on Saturday morning, my problem was not solved. Now my serious cry was for the Lord to show if it was my duty to break silence and speak to my employer. Should I continue to wait for the Lord's time? After much prayer, I felt that it was best to wait for His time. I was sure that God would help me in some way. So I waited, my heart at rest.

At about five o'clock that Saturday afternoon, the doctor had finished his paperwork and completed his last duties for the day. Sitting in his big chair, he began to speak of the things of God. He was truly a Christian man and we had many very happy spiritual visits together. I was doing a medical test and boiling a pan of water. It was very good for me to be so busy.

All at once he said, "Tell me, Taylor, is it not time for your pay again?" You can imagine my feelings! I had to swallow two or three times before I could answer. With my eyes on the pan and my back to the doctor, I told him as quietly as I could that it was due some time ago. How thankful I felt! God had heard my prayer. He had caused my employer to remember the pay without any word from me.

He answered, "Oh, I am so sorry you did not remind me! You know how busy I am. I wish I had thought of it sooner, for only this afternoon I sent all the money to the bank. Otherwise I would pay you at once."

It is impossible to describe the terrible feeling caused by these unexpected words. I did not know what to do. Just at that time my pan boiled and I had good reason to leave the room with it. I was pleased to get away and keep out of sight until after the doctor had returned to his house. I was very thankful that he had not seen my sad feeling.

As soon as he was gone I found a place to pray and poured out my heart before the Lord. Soon, a sense of calmness, thankfulness and happiness came back to my heart. I felt that God had His own way and was not going to fail me. I had prayed to know His will early in the day. As far as I could judge, guidance had come for me to wait quietly. Now God was going to work for me in some other way.

As usual, I spent that Saturday evening alone reading the Bible and preparing to preach in the usual lodging houses[G] on the next day. I waited a little longer than usual. At last, about ten o'clock, I put on my coat and was preparing to leave for home. I was thankful to know that by the time I arrived, the landlady would already be in bed. There was certainly no help for that night. Still, God may bring help for me by Monday enabling me to pay what I owed for my room early in the week.

As I was preparing to turn off the gas light, I heard the doctor's footsteps in the garden between his house and the office. He was laughing to himself as he entered and asked for the record book, telling me that a very unusual thing had happened. A rich man had just come to pay his bill. What an unusual time this was to go out to pay a bill. It did not come to my mind that it might have anything to do with my own problem. It might have made me feel ashamed.

But it made me laugh to think about a man who was rolling in wealth, coming after ten o'clock at night to pay a doctor's bill. He could have done this easily in the morning. It seemed that somehow he could not rest with this on his mind and felt that he must come at that unusual hour to pay what he owed.

The amount was written in the record book. As he was about to leave, the doctor turned quickly and gave me some of the money. To my surprise and thankfulness, he said "By the way, Taylor, you should take this money. I do not have any change, but I can give you the rest next week." Again I was left - my feelings undiscovered - to praise the Lord with a happy heart that after all I might be able to go to China. To me, the thing was not a small matter. In difficult situations, thinking of it has given great spiritual rest and strength.

Soon, the time came for me to leave Hull and receive medical training at the London Hospital. After a short time there, I had every reason to believe that my lifework in China would begin. I was very happy because of the willingness of God to hear and answer prayer. He showed himself more than willing to help His half-trusting and frightened child. But I felt that I could not go to China without more work in developing and testing my power to rest upon His faithfulness. Soon, a special chance was given to me.

My father had offered to pay for my stay in London. I knew that because of recent losses, it would mean a real sacrifice for him to meet this cost. This came just when it seemed necessary for me to go forward. I had recently come to know the Committee of the Chinese Evangelisation Society[G] under which I finally left for China. I had met its able leader Mr. George Pearse who became my much loved friend. He worked for the Stock Exchange.[2]

Not knowing of my father's offer, the Committee was also kindly prepared to pay for my stay in London. When these offers were first made, I was not clear as to what I should to do. I wrote to my father and the Chinese Evangelisation Society leaders, advising that I would take a few days of prayer before deciding the path to follow. I told them of the offers that each had made.

While waiting upon God for guidance, it became clear that it would be easy to refuse both offers. The leaders of the society would not know that I had put myself wholly on God for my needs. At the same time, my father would think that I had accepted the other offer. I wrote and kindly refused both, feeling that without anyone to worry about my needs, I was simply in the hands of God. I felt that the Lord knew my heart and wished to send me to China. He would bless my effort at home to depend upon Him alone.

[1] Society: an organized group working together because of a common belief.
[2] Stock Exchange: where company shares are bought and sold.

CHAPTER FIVE

# Life In London

I must not try to tell all the ways in which the Lord was pleased to help me from time to time. To my surprise and great joy it happened often. I soon found that it was not possible to live on as little money in London as it was in Hull. To cut costs, a cousin and I rented one room and lived together, four miles from the hospital. In preparing my food, I tried different things. I found that eating brown bread and water would save a considerable amount of my wages.

In this way, I was able to make God's money last as long as possible. Some of my living costs could not be reduced, but my choice of food enabled me to save some money. Each day on my long walk home from the hospital, I bought a large piece of brown bread for two pennies[G]. I ate this for supper and breakfast. On that food and a little fruit for lunch, I walked eight or nine miles a day and was on my feet much of the time at the hospital and medical school.

I must tell my readers about one thing that happened just about this time. The husband of my landlady in Hull was chief officer of a ship that sailed from London. By getting his half pay monthly and sending it to her, I was able save her the cost that the bank would charge. I had been doing this for several months when she wrote asking that I get the next payment as early as possible, as her rent was almost due. She depended upon that amount to pay it.

By working hard for a test, I was hoping to get a gift for school fees which would help me. I was unwilling to waste time by going to the city during the busiest part of the day. I had enough of my own money to send what she needed. So, I sent it to her, planning to go later and get her money and repay myself.

Before the test, the medical school was closed for a day to mark the funeral of the Duke of Wellington. This gave me a chance to go to the office near Cheapside and collect the pay. To my unhappy surprise, the man at the office told me that he could not pay it, because the officer had run away from his ship and gone to dig gold. "Well," I said, "that is not good at all for me because I have already sent the money. I know his wife will have no way to pay me back."

The man at the office said he was sorry but could only do as he was told. There was no help for me in that direction. A little more time and prayer brought the peaceful thought to my mind that I was depending on the Lord for everything. His ways were not limited. It was a small thing to be brought into the position of bringing my needs to Him. The happiness and peace in my heart were not troubled for very long.

Soon after this, while putting together some writing paper for school, I accidentally stuck the first finger of my right hand. However, the pain soon went away and I forgot all about it. The next day at the hospital I continued to operate as before. A person had died of a dangerous sickness that caused high temperature. The body was more than usually offensive and dangerous. Those who worked upon it operated with special care, knowing that the smallest cut might cost our lives.

Before the morning was half over, I began to feel very tired. At about noon, I had to run out to throw up. This was most unusual for me, as I ate little food and nothing that could make me sick. Feeling very weak for some time, I found a drink of cold water helped me to feel better, enabling me to return to work. Yet, the sickness increased and before the afternoon class was over, I found it impossible to continue taking notes. Before long, there was severe pain in my whole arm and right side. I was becoming very sick.

Unable to continue work, I went into the operating room to close up the body I was working on and put away my tools. I advised the teacher, a skilled surgeon[G] that I was sick but was not sure of the cause. He told me that I had cut myself. To my surprise, he said that I had caught the sickness that killed the person on which I had been operating.

I told him that I had been most careful and was very certain that I had no cut or broken skin. "Well," he said, "you certainly must have had one." He looked very closely at my hand but found no break in my skin. Then, I recalled that I had stuck my finger the night before and asked if it were possible that this wound could still have been open. He confirmed that this was the probable cause of the trouble. He advised that I get home as fast as I could to close my personal business. "For," he said, "you are a dead man."

I was hit with a feeling of sorrow that I could not go to China. Yet, very soon came the feeling, that unless I was greatly mistaken, I had work to do in China and would not die. I talked to this medical friend, who did not believe in God or spiritual things. I talked of happiness in the possibility of soon being with my Master. I expressed the belief that I would not die. Unless I were much mistaken, I had work to do in China and must not lose the battle.

"That is all very well," he answered, "but you get a hansom[G] and go home as fast as you can. You have no time to lose, for you will soon be unable to finish up your personal business." I smiled at the idea of going home in a hansom. By this time there was too little of my money left to allow such a thing. So, I tried to walk home. It was not long before my strength gave way and it was useless to attempt to continue. I rode on a large bus from Whitechapel Church to Farringdon Street and another from Farringdon Street on towards home.

In great suffering, I reached my home near Soho Square. Immediately, I got some hot water from the servant. I was as direct as my coming death would allow. Speaking to her very strongly, I advised her to accept salvation through Jesus Christ as the gift of God. Pouring water over my head, I cut open the finger, hoping to let out some of the poisoned blood. The pain was very severe and I passed out for some time. On awaking, I found that I had been carried to bed.

I had an uncle who lived nearby. He came in and sent for his own doctor, an assistant surgeon[G] at the Westminster Hospital. I told him that medical help would be of little use to me. I did not wish to spend the money that it would cost. He quieted me on this point, saying that he had sent for his own doctor and he would pay the bill. The surgeon examined me and said, "Well, if you have been living a clean life and without rich foods, you may pull through. But if you have been going in for strong drink and that sort of thing, there would be no chance at all for you."

I thought that if a clean life without rich food was to do anything, few could have a better chance. Little more than bread and water had been my only food for a long time. I told him I had lived very much that way and found that it helped my study. "But now," he said, "you must keep up your strength, for it will be a very hard battle." He said I needed a bottle of port wine[G] every day and as much good meat as I could eat. Again I smiled to myself, having no money to buy such rich food. This difficulty was met by my kind uncle who immediately sent me all that was needed.

I was in great pain, but still did not want my parents to know that I was sick. Thinking and praying about it caused me to believe that I was not going to die, because there truly was work for me to do in China. If my parents came up and found me in that condition, I would lose the chance to see how God was going to work for me, now that my money had almost come to an end.

After prayer for guidance, my uncle and cousin promised not to write to them, but to let me inform them myself. I felt it was a very clear answer to prayer when they gave me this promise. I took care to wait until the crisis was well past and the most severe part of the sickness was over. Only then did I let them know. At home, they knew that I was working hard for a test and did not wonder at my silence.

Days and nights of suffering passed slowly by. After several weeks, I was strong enough to leave my room. I learned that two men working at another hospital had died of this same kind of sickness. I had been protected in answer to prayer to work for God in China.

[1] Surgeon: a doctor who operates or does surgery.

[2] Hansom: a hire car pulled by a horse.

[3] Wine: a drink made from grapes.

CHAPTER SIX

# Strengthened By Faith

One day the doctor came in and found me sitting in a chair. He was surprised to learn that with help, I had walked downstairs. He advised that I should get off to the country as soon as I was well enough and stay there to regain health and strength. To begin work too soon would cause the sickness to come again with serious results.

I was very tired and weak. When he had left, I prayed to the Lord about how I was keeping my sickness secret from those who would be very happy to help me. I told Him I was trying to strengthen my faith by depending on Him. What was I to do? I waited for His answer.

It seemed as if He were directing me to go again to the shipping office to ask about the pay I had been unable to draw. I reminded Him that I did not have money to go by public transport and may not be able to get my pay. I asked if this was not just my idea to get some money and not His guidance and teaching. After prayer and more waiting, I was sure that He wanted me to go to the office.

I had to come downstairs and then walk over two miles. Certain of receiving whatever I requested of God, I asked Him for strength to make the long walk. Sending the servant for my hat and stick, I set out for Cheapside expecting God's help.

Without question, I was strengthened by faith. Yet, I never took as much interest in store windows as I did on that trip. At every second or third step I was happy to rest a little against the glass and look in. A special effort of faith was needed when I got to Farringdon Street to attempt the hard climb of Snow Hill. There was no Holborn Bridge in those days.

God helped me wonderfully. In time, I reached the office in Cheapside and sat down on the steps leading to the first floor. The business men hurried up and down the stairs looking at me with questioning eyes. After rest and more prayer, I climbed the stairs and was happy to find the man who had earlier spoken to me about the money.

Seeing me looking so colourless and weak, he asked about my health. I said that I was to go to the country but first wanted to check on the man who had run off to dig gold. He smiled, advising me that there was a mistake made with another man of the same name. It appeared that the man was still on the ship and due to return to port within a day or two. He was happy to give me the half-pay to make sure that it would reach the wife safely. He knew of the temptations that attack the men when they arrive home after a long time at sea.

He invited me to come inside to eat part of his lunch. It was truly the Lord helping me and I thankfully accepted his offer. Having eaten and rested, I was given a piece of paper on which to write, advising the wife of the situation. On my way back, I mailed a money order for the amount due to her. After that, I felt that it was not a waste of money to ride a bus home.

Feeling very much better the next morning, I walked to the surgery of the doctor who had attended me. I had decided that it was not right for my uncle to pay my bills now that I had the money. The kind surgeon[G] refused to charge a medical student for his work. He allowed me to pay for the quinine[G] he had given me. After that, the remaining money was just enough to take me home. It proved to me the work of God in my life.

Knowing that the surgeon claimed not to believe in God, I asked if I could speak to him freely. Advising that through God I owed my life to his kind care, I wished him the same faith in God that I had. I told him of my reason for being in London, my plans to go to China and my refusal of help from my father and the leaders of the mission. I told him of the way God had taken care of me and how hopeless my position had been the day before, when he had advised that I go to the country.

I told him of the battle in my mind and that I had walked all the way from my house to Cheapside. Looking with disbelief, he told me that he had left me more like a spirit than a man. I had to tell him again and again that my faith gave me the strength to make the walk. Advising him of the money now in hand, I explained that just enough was left to go home to Yorkshire and buy food on the way.

My kind friend was completely broken down and told me with tears in his eyes that he would give all the world for a faith like mine. With great joy, I said that it was to be gotten without money. We never met again. On my return to town, I found that he had suffered a stroke[2] and had died. I was able to learn nothing about his spiritual condition on his death, but have always felt thankful that I had the chance to tell him of God. I can only hope that the Master was speaking to him through me and that we shall meet again in the Better Land. It would be wonderful to be welcomed by him when my own work is over.

The next day found me in my parent's home. My joy in the Lord's help was so great that I was unable to keep my secret to myself. Before my return to London, my mother knew of what had been happening in my life. After that, I was not allowed to live on the same kind of food as before my sickness. I needed more now and the Lord provided.

[1] Quinine: a kind of medicine.
[2] Stroke: a sudden attack of sickness, often causing death.

CHAPTER SEVEN

# Mighty to Save

With the return of my health, I went back to London to start my schooling again. My busy study life was continued, often eased by happy Sundays with Christian friends. I found chances for service in every place. There was one case that gave me great faith in seeking the salvation of another.

God had given me the joy of winning souls before, but not in a place of special difficulty. With God all things are possible. No salvation ever takes place except by the unlimited power of the Holy Spirit. For this reason, the great need of every Christian worker is to "know" God. Truly, this is the purpose for which He has given us everlasting life, as our Saviour Himself says, in John 17:3 *"Now this is eternal life: that they may know you, the only true God, and Jesus Christ, whom you have sent."*

I was now to prove the willingness of God to answer prayer for spiritual blessing under the most unpromising situation. Because of this, I gained a greater understanding of the prayer-answering God as One *"mighty to save."* (Zephaniah 3:17)

A short time before leaving for China, it became my daily duty to change the bandage[G] of a man suffering from a poisoned foot. The disease started as usual, its deadliness not easy to see. The man had little idea that he must die within a short time. I was not the first to attend to him, but when the case was given to me, I became very concerned about his soul.

His family was Christian, but he was not and hostile to any talk of God. Without asking him, they had asked a Scripture reader to visit. In great anger, the man had ordered him to leave. The local pastor had also called, hoping to help him. But the man had spat in his face. His anger was very fierce, making help seem very hopeless.

I prayed much about my planned visits to him. For two or three days, I said nothing about his soul. By special care, I was able to greatly ease his sufferings and he began to be thankful for my help. One day, with a fearful heart, I took the chance to tell him of what guided my life and the need for God's mercy through Christ. Only by the power of his self-control did he keep his mouth closed. He turned over in bed with his back to me and did not speak.

I could not get the poor man out of my mind. Each day, I called on God to save the man before he died. When changing the bandage to ease his pain, I never failed to say a few words which I hoped the Lord would bless. The man always turned his back to me, looking angry, but never answering a word.

After some time, my heart sank. It seemed that I was doing no good and was even hardening his heart and making him more guilty. One day, after caring for him, I stopped at the door and thought, *"Ephraim is joined to his idols;*[G] *let him alone."* (Hosea 4:17) I looked at the man and saw his surprise, as it was the first time that I had left without going to his bedside to say a few words for my Master.

I could wait no longer. Breaking into tears, I walked over to him saying, "My friend, you may or may not listen to me. Yet, I *must* tell you what is in *my* heart." I went on to speak very seriously to him, telling him how much I wished that he would let me pray with him. To my great joy he answered, "If it will be a help to you, do it." I fell on my knees and poured out my whole soul to God for him. At that point, I believe the Lord made a change in his soul.

After this, he was always willing to be spoken to and prayed with. Within a few days, he accepted Christ as his Saviour. What a joy it was for me to see that man full of praise and happiness in hope of the glory of God! He told me that for forty years, he had never gone through the door of a church. He had only entered a place of worship to be married. Later, he would not even go inside for the funeral of his wife.

Thank God, I believe that his sin-marked soul was now washed and completely given to God, through the name of the Lord Jesus Christ. During my early work in China, many situations have given me a deep sense of hopeless. I have thought of this man's salvation and been strengthened to continue speaking the Word, if men listened or not.

The happy sufferer lived for some time and was never tired of giving witness to the grace of God. Though his condition was very sad, this change in his life made my labour one of joy. I have often thought of the words, "He who goes out weeping,[G] carrying seed to sow,[G] will return with songs of joy, carrying sheaves[G] with him."

We should all have that extreme hunger for souls that leads to tears. Then, we should more often see the victory we desire. Sometimes we may speak unhappily of the hardness of the hearts of those we seek to see saved. The true cause of our failure may be the hardness of our own hearts and our own weak understanding of the serious truth of heaven and hell.

[1] Bandage: the covering put on a wound.
[2] Idol: an object to worship, a false god.
[3] Weep: cry with sorrow.
[4] Sow: to plant.
[5] Sheaves: wheat or other grain plants that have been gathered and fastened.

CHAPTER EIGHT

# Ocean Trip to China

At last, the time came for me to leave England for China. I had looked forward to this for a long time. I left London for Liverpool to go on the *Dumfries,* booked for me by the Committee of the Chinese Evangelisation Society,[G] under whose care I was going to China. On September 19, 1853, a service was held in my small sleeping room at the back end of the ship.

My beloved mother had come to see me off from Liverpool. I shall never forget that day. She went with me into the little room that was to be my home for nearly six long months. With a mother's loving hand, she prepared the little bed. Sitting by my side, she joined me in the last Gospel song that we would sing together before I left home for a very long time. We knelt and she prayed. It was the last mother's prayer I was to hear before starting for China. The time then came for us to separate and we had to say good-bye, never expecting to meet on earth again.

She controlled her feelings as much as possible. We parted and she left the ship, giving me her blessing. I stood alone on the deck,[G] and she followed the ship as we moved toward the end of the wharf. As the ship moved away, the separation really began. I shall never forget the cry of pain that was torn from that mother's heart. It went through me like a knife. I never knew so fully the meaning of "God so loved the world." I am sure that in that hour, my beloved mother depended more on the love of God than she had ever done in her life.

Oh, what sorrow it must give the heart of God when He sees His children not caring about the needs of the wide world for which His beloved and only Son died!

*"Listen, O daughter, consider and give ear: Forget your people and your father's house. The king will greatly desire your beauty; honor him, for he is your lord."* Psalms 45:10-11

Praise God, there is a growing number of people finding the joys given to those who follow Him. They empty their hearts of their own will and leave all to obey Him in the great work of spreading the Gospel.

On September 19, 1853, the *Dumfries* sailed for China. We arrived in Shanghai on March 1, in the spring of the following year. Our voyage had a rough beginning, but many had promised to remember us in continuous prayer. This was a great help for we had just left the Mersey River when a fierce seasonal wind caught us. For twelve days, we were sailing up and down in the Irish Channel, unable to get out to sea.

The wind continued to increase and after almost a week, we were able to hide behind some land. But soon we had to raise the sails again and try to sail off into the wind. The greatest efforts of the captain[G] and crew was useless. Sunday night found us being pushed into Carnarvon Bay, each tack[2] becoming shorter, until at last we were sailing very close to the rocks along the land.

About this time, as the ship was put round in the other direction, the Christian captain said to me, "We cannot live half an hour now. What of your call to labor for the Lord in China?" Before, I had passed through a time of great conflict, but that was over. It was a great joy to tell him that I would not for any amount of money be in any other position. I informed him that I surely expected to reach China. If not, the Master would be pleased that I was seeking to obey His command.

Within a few minutes, the captain told me that the wind had changed two points, enabling us to sail out to sea. And so we did. Many parts of the boat were damaged, but in a few days we moved into open sea. The necessary repairs were made as we sailed so that our trip to China was not slowed down.

One thing was a great trouble to me that night. I was a very young believer and did not have enough faith in God to see Him working through the use of things. I had felt it a duty to obey my beloved and honoured mother and to please her I bought a life preserver.[3] But in my own soul, I felt as if I could not simply trust in God while I had this life preserver. All hope of our ship being saved was gone. However, my heart had no rest until I gave it away.

Then with perfect peace, I put several light things together, likely to float at the time we would run into the rocks. I had no thought of wrongdoing and was not troubled that my actions and words did not agree. Ever since, I have seen clearly the mistake I made. It is one that is very common in these days, when false teaching on faith healing does much harm. It leads some to make mistakes about the purposes of God, shakes the faith of others, and troubles the minds of many. The use of things should not weaken our faith in God. Also, our faith in God should not stop us from using whatever means are at hand to complete the work He has given.

For years after this, I always took a life preserver with me and my mind was never troubled about it. After the storm was over, the question was settled for me, through the prayerful study of the Scriptures. God led me to see my mistake, probably to free me from a great deal of trouble on similar questions now so often asked. In medical work, I have always asked for God's guidance and blessing in the use of tools and medicine and then been careful to give Him thanks for answered prayer and renewed health. But to me it would seem foolish and wrong to fail to use those things which He has put within our reach. In the same way, we would be unwise not to take daily food and think that we could have life and health by prayer alone.

The ocean trip was a very unexciting one. Calm weather made us lose much time on the equator[G] and through the Eastern Archipelago. Usually a light wind would spring up soon after the sun went down and last until daybreak. Our captain[G] would make the most use of it. During the day, we lay still with empty sails. Often, the wind would blow us back and rob us of a good part of the distance we had gained during the night.

At one time, we were dangerously close to the north of New Guinea. Saturday night had brought us to a point some 45 to 50 kilometres off the land. During the Sunday morning service, I could not fail to see that the captain looked troubled, often going over to the side of the ship. Later, I learned from him that the current was carrying us quickly towards some under-water reefs.[5] We were already so near that it seemed unlikely that we should get through the afternoon in safety. After dinner, the long-boat was put out and all hands tried to turn the ship from the land, but were not able to.

As we stood together in silence, the captain said, "Well, we have done everything that can be done and we can only wait for the results."

I said, "No, there is one thing we have not done yet."

"What is it?" he asked.

"Four of us on the ship are Christians," I answered. "Let us each go to our own room and pray, asking the Lord to give us a wind. He can as easily send it now as after the sun goes down."

The captain agreed. I spoke to the other two men. After prayer together, we went to our rooms to wait upon God. I had a good but short time in prayer. Feeling so satisfied that our request would be given, I could not continue asking, but went up on the deck[G]. The first officer, a godless man, was in charge. I asked him to let down the clews[6] of the mainsail, which had been pulled up to stop the useless moving of the sail against the rigging.[7]

He asked why we would want to do that. I told him we had been asking for a wind from God and that it was coming soon. We were so near the reef that there was not a minute to lose. He looked at me as if I were insane and swore that it was better to see a wind than hear of it! But I watched his eye and followed it up to the royal,[8] and there, the edge of the sail was beginning to move in the coming wind.

"Don't you see the wind is coming? Look at the royal!" I said excitedly. "No, it is only a cat's-paw,[9]" he said.

"Cat's-paw or not," I called, "please let down the mainsail and let us have the good from it!"

This he was not slow to do. In another minute, there was the loud sound of the crew running on the deck. This brought the captain up from his room to find that the wind had come. In a few minutes, we were making our way through the water pushed by a nice wind and were soon out of danger. Though the wind was sometimes not strong, we did not lose it until after passing the Pelew Islands.

In this way, God helped my faith to grow. Before landing in China, I learned to bring every kind of need to Him in prayer and to expect that He would honour the name of the Lord Jesus and give the help needed.

[1] Deck: floor of a ship.

[2] Tack: the way sailboats must sail first one way and then the other to sail into the wind.

[3] Life Preserver: something worn to make a person float in water.
[4] Equator: the area around the middle part of the world.
[5] Reef: stone-like growth.
[6] Clew: corner of a sail.
[7] Rigging: supporting ropes.
[8] Royal: the topmost sail.
[9] Cat's-paw: one small bit of wind.

# CHAPTER NINE

# Early Missionary Experiences

On landing in Shanghai on March 1, 1854, I found myself circled with difficulties that were completely unexpected. A group of rebels, known as the "Red Turbans," had taken possession of the city. A government army of forty to fifty thousand men had come to fight. This army gave more trouble to the small European population than the rebels did.

Upon landing, I was told that it was impossible to live out of the European settlement.[1] Within this area, there were no flats or rooms to rent at any price. The dollar[G] which was worth about three shillings, had risen to a value of eight and ninepence. The outlook was very dark for one with only a small income of English money. However, I had three letters from friends in England to bring to their friends in Shanghai asking them to help me. I was depending on these for help and advice, especially from one whose friends I knew well and highly valued. I looked for this friend at once, only to learn that he had recently died.

Saddened by this news, I searched for a missionary to whom another of my letters was written. But to my sorrow, I found that he had left for America. The third letter had been given to me by a person I did not know well. I had expected less from it than from the other two. Yet, it proved to be God's way for help. The letter was written to Rev. Dr. Medhurst, of the London Mission. He took me to meet Dr. Lockhart who kindly allowed me to live with him for six months. Dr. Medhurst helped me find my first Chinese teacher who with Dr. Edkins and the late Mr. Alexander Wylie gave me considerable help with the language.

Those were truly trouble filled and dangerous times. One day I was coming out of the city with Mr. Wylie when he began talking to two carriers. We had been waiting for a friend at the East Gate. An attack was made on the city by groups of soldiers on the opposite side of the river, causing us to hurry away to a place of less danger. We could hear the sound of the cannonballs[G] that came flying over our heads.

The carriers stayed too long and were wounded. On reaching the settlement, we went at once to the London Mission compound.[G] At the door of the hospital, we found the two carriers with their feet terribly smashed by a cannonball. They refused to allow their feet to be removed and both soon died. We felt how close our escape had been.

Early one morning, I had joined a missionary on his veranda[G] to watch a fierce battle at a distance of two kilometres. All at once, a spent cannonball passed between us and buried itself in the veranda wall. Another day, Mr. Wylie was sitting on a chair. He left for a few minutes and upon returning, found the arm of the chair broken off completely by a cannonball. But in the middle of such dangers, God protected us.

After my stay of six months with Dr. Lockhart, I rented a house outside the settlement and began missionary work among my Chinese neighbours as long as the war allowed. When the French joined the government army in attacking the city, the position of my house became very dangerous. During the last few weeks, the fighting prevented me from sleeping, except in the daytime.

One night, a fire appeared very near. I climbed up to a little place on the top of the house to see if it was necessary to escape. A cannonball hit the top edge of the roof of the next house, throwing pieces of broken roof tile[6] all around me. The ball rolled down into the court below. It was heavy and could easily have hit me. I sent it to my mother who kept it for many years. Before long, I had to return to the European settlement. I left just in time because, not long after, the house was burned to the ground. It is not possible to show any true picture of the frightfulness of this war. A gentle person would find the terrors, wrongs and sorrow to be terrible things.

I was also very ashamed because of the lack of money. My income was eighty pounds a year. The need to pay one hundred twenty for the house, forced me to rent out half of it. After Dr. Parker came, the Committee of the Chinese Evangelisation Society[G] learned more of the situation and increased my income. But many painful times had been passed through. Few realise how troubling these difficulties were to an inexperienced worker or the great loneliness of starting such new work. It was not a matter one could tell friends at home without appearing to be shamefully asking for help.

The great enemy was always to believe that *"Everything is against me!"* (Genesis 42:36) But, how false the word! The cold, the hunger, the watchings and sleepless nights added to feelings of complete aloneness and helplessness. All of this was wisely chosen by God and gently and lovingly measured out to me. What situations could have made the Word of God sweeter, the nearness of God so real and the help of God so priceless? They were truly times of pouring out self and I saw the smallness of our true value. Yet that did not make me feel ashamed (Romans 5:5). It strengthened my purpose to go forward as God might direct, with His proven promise, *"I will be with you. I will never leave you or give up on you."* (Joshua 1:5)

One can see, even now, that *"as for God, his way is perfect,"* (Psalms 18:30). Yet, we can be thankful that the missionary path of today is a much smoother and easier one.

The agreement between the Chinese and British governments did not include foreigners travelling inland[G]. This was done with much difficulty, especially for some time after the Battle of Muddy Flat. An American group of about three hundred soldiers, with fewer than a hundred men from the settlement, attacked and drove off an army of the thirty to fifty thousand government soldiers. Their guns would shoot much farther than those of the Chinese. Still, in the autumn of 1854, I safely made a week long trip with Dr. Edkins. He did the speaking and preaching while I passed out the Gospel books and tracts.

[1] Settlement: the Settlement spoken of here was an area in Shanghai set aside for Europeans to live. This area was done away with in 1943.
[2] Dollar: the name of money used by several countries.
[3] Cannon: a very large gun.
[4] Compound: *1* to mix or put together; *2* a walled or closed-in area. Meaning *2* used here.
[5] Veranda: an open room on the outside of a building.
[6] Roof tile: a baked red dirt (clay) roof material.

# CHAPTER TEN

# First Evangelistic Efforts

In the spring of 1855, I took a somewhat dangerous trip with the Rev. J. S. Burdon of the Church Missionary Society.[G] He later became the Bishop[1] of Victoria, Hong Kong. In the great mouth of the River Yangtze, about thirty miles to the north of Shanghai, is the group of islands of which Tsungming and Haimen[2] are the largest and most important. Up river is the important city of Tungchow, close to Lang-shan, or Wolf Mountains, famous as a holiday place for those who worship evil spirits.

We spent some time in bringing the Good News to those islands and then went on to Lang-shan. Here we preached and gave books to thousands of the worshipers attending a special holiday for those who worship evil spirits. From there we went on to Tungchow, The following from my diary[G] will tell of our painful time there:

Thursday, April 26, 1855

After breakfast, we prayed and placed ourselves in the care of our heavenly Father, asking for His blessing before we went to this great city. The day was cloudy and wet. We felt sure that Satan would not allow us to attack his area without a very serious fight. We also knew that it was the will of God that we preach Christ in this city and give the Word of truth to its people. We were sorry that we had but few books left for such an important place. The result later proved that this showed God's watchfulness over us.

Our national teachers did their best to tell us not to go into the city. But we had decided that, by God's help, nothing should stop us. We told them to stay in one of the boats. If we did not return, they were to learn what they could about what happened and return quickly to Shanghai to tell our friends. We also asked that the other boat wait for us, even if we could not get back that night. Taking our books and a worker, we set off for the city, about seven miles away. Walking was out of the question because the roads were very muddy. So we rode in wheelbarrows,[G] the only transportation in these areas. Needing only one carrier, this was less costly but not a nice way to travel on rough, dirty roads.

We had not gone far before the worker asked to go back, as he was completely frightened by reports about the national soldiers. We told him to return, not wanting to involve another in trouble and decided to carry the books ourselves. We looked to Him for extra strength, for our body as well as spiritual strength, who had promised to provide all our needs.

At this point, a kind and important looking man came up and seriously warned us against going on. He said that if we did, we should find to our sorrow what the Tungchow soldiers were like. We thanked him for his kind warning, but could not act upon it as our hearts were fixed. We did not know if we were facing prison and death or to pass out Scriptures and tracts safely. But we had decided, by the grace of God, not to leave Tungchow any longer without the Gospel. We did not want its many thousands of citizens to die not knowing of the love of God.

After this, my wheelbarrow[G] man would go no nearer the city. I found another with little difficulty. As we went on in the mud and rain, we could not help feeling the danger of our position, but our minds did not change. From time to time we strengthened each other with Scripture and singing Gospel songs. I recall one such song which seemed to fit our situation very well and make me feel much better.

> The dangers of the sea, the dangers of the land,
> Should not frighten you: your Lord is near at hand.
> But should your fearlessness fail, when tried andstrongly
>     troubled,
> His promise shall stand true, and set your soul at rest

We passed through one small town of about a thousand souls. In the Mandarin language, I preached Jesus to a good number of people. Never was I so happy in speaking of the love of God and the atonement of Jesus Christ. My own soul was richly blessed and filled with joy and peace. I was able to speak with unusual ease.

How happy I was when, after preaching, I heard one of our listeners repeating to newcomers, the truths of which I had spoken.

Oh, how thankful I felt to hear a Chinese telling his friend that God loved them, that they were sinners, but that Jesus died instead of them and paid for their guilt! That one time was worth all the trials we had passed through. I felt that if the Lord should give His Holy Spirit to change the heart of that man, we had not come for nothing.

We passed out a few New Testaments and tracts for the people were able to read. We could not leave them without the Gospel. It was well that we did so, for when we reached Tungchow we found we were so tired that we were pleased to have only a light load.

Nearing the end of our trip, at the west side of the city, I recalled the prayer of the early Christians, when mistreatment was starting. *"And now, Lord, consider their threats, and enable your servants to speak your word with great fearlessness."* (Acts 4:29) In this prayer we fully joined with the early Christians. Before entering the edge of town, we made our plans so that we could act together. We informed our wheelbarrow[G] men where to wait for us, so that they would not get into any of our trouble. Then, looking up to our heavenly Father, we placed ourselves in His keeping, took our books and set off for the city.

We walked along the road to the West Gate and smiled at the unusual name of heh-kwei-tsi (black spirits) which was given to us. We wondered about it but later found that it was our clothes that caused them to use this name for us. Passing several soldiers, I said to Mr. Burdon that these were the men we had heard so much about. They seemed willing to receive us quietly enough.

Long before reaching the gate, a tall powerful man made fierce by drink stopped us. He roughly held Mr. Burdon, letting us know that all the soldiers were not so peacefully minded. My friend tried to shake him off. As I turned to see what the trouble was, we were encircled by twelve or more cruel looking men who hurried us on to the city.

Soon, my load became more than I could carry and I was unable to change hands to help myself. I was soon very hot and hardly able to keep up with them. We demanded to be taken before the chief judge but were told that they knew where to take us and what to do with people like us. They spoke to us using most insulting names.

The fierce, drunken man soon left Mr. Burdon and became my chief troubler. I was neither as tall nor strong as my friend and was less able to stand against the man. He hit me and almost made me fall down again and again. Taking me roughly by the hair, he held my clothes around my neck and almost stopped my breath completely. He held me hard around my arms and the top of my body making these parts black and blue. Had this treatment continued much longer, I would have passed out. With my strength almost gone, it was a joy to remember a few lines about heaven that my mother wrote in her last letter to me:

We speak of the home of the blest,
That country so bright and so fair,
And often are its glories confessed;
But what must it be to be there!

To be gone from the body! To be present with the Lord! To be free from sin! This is the end of all that man's evil can ever bring upon us.

As we walked along, Mr. Burdon tried to give away a few books, not knowing if we might have another chance to do so. But the soldier became angry and demanded that handcuffs[4] be brought. None could be found, but this showed us that we could do no good in trying to pass out books. There was nothing to be done but quietly obey and go with the soldiers.

One or two times, they argued about what should be done with us. One said that we should be taken to the judge's office, but others wanted to kill us at once without appeal to any government officer. We were at peace, recalling that the apostles[G] were happy to be thought honorable enough to feel pain for the cause of Christ.

From my pocket, I took a Chinese name card. I demanded that we be led to office of the chief official and the card be presented to him. After this, we were treated with more honour. Before this, we had been unable to make them understand that we were foreigners although we wore English clothes.

Oh, we were roughly pulled through many long tiring roads that did not seem to end. I have never felt more thankful than when we stopped at the house where a mandarin[G] lived. We were both very tired and in serious need of a drink of water. Resting against a wall, I asked them to bring us something to sit on, but they told us to wait. On begging them to give us something to drink, I received the same answer. Around the doorway, a large crowd had gathered. Collecting his remaining strength, Mr. Burdon preached Jesus Christ. The cards and books had been taken in to the mandarin. Since he was a low level official, he finally sent us to a higher officer.

Finding that they planned to turn us out again into the crowded roads, we refused to move one step and demanded that sedans[G] be brought. This was done after some dispute and we were carried off. On the road, we felt so thankful for the chance to rest and for having preached Jesus in the face of Satan's evil efforts. Our joy must have showed on our faces. As we passed along, we heard some say that we did not look like bad men. Others seemed to feel sorry for us.

On arrival at the judge's office, I wondered where we were being taken. We had passed through great doors that looked like those of the city wall, but we were still within the city. We entered a second door which made it appear to be a prison. But on seeing a large sign made of stone, with the words "Ming chi fu mu" (the father and mother of the people), we felt that we had been carried to the right place, this being the official name used by the mandarins.

Our cards were again sent in. After a short delay, we were taken in to see Ch'en Ta Lao-ie (the Great Honorable Father Ch'en), who had been Tao-tai of Shanghai. He knew the importance of treating foreigners with kindness. Coming before him, some of the people fell on their knees and put their heads down to the ground. My guard motioned me to do the same, but I did not obey.

This mandarin seemed to be the highest official of Tungchow and wore a solid blue button on his hat. He came out and treated us with every possible sign of honour. He took us to a more private room, but we were followed by many writers, runners and other low officials. I explained the reason for our visit and begged to be allowed to give him copies of our books and tracts, for which he thanked me. Giving him a copy of the New Testament with part of the Old (from Genesis to Ruth), I made a short explanation of our teachings. He listened very carefully, as did all the others present. He then ordered food which he ate with us.

After a long stay, we asked to be permitted to see something of the city. Before leaving, we wanted to hand out the books we had brought. He kindly agreed. We said we had earlier been most dishonourably treated. We told him we understood that the soldiers knew no better. However, we asked him to give orders that we were not to be troubled any more.

This he promised to do and with every possible sign of honour, walked with us to the door of his official home. Several runners were sent to ensure that we were treated with honour. We handed out our books and left the city. It was interesting to see the way in which the runners made use of their queues.[8] When the road was blocked by the crowd, they used these to hit the people.

We found our wheelbarrows[G] and paid off the sedan[G] carriers. Then we sat on our simple transports and returned to the river. We were followed for half the distance by a worker from the judge's office. Early in the evening we got back to the boats in safety, truly thankful to our heavenly Father for His gracious protection and aid.

[1] Bishop: a leader of pastors and their churches.

[2] The island of Haimen disappeared many years later when the Yangtze River changed its course and was joined with the northern bank of the river.

[3] Wheelbarrow: a box-like tool with one wheel and two handles, for moving small loads.

[4] Handcuffs: a thing made of metal to fasten ones hands together.

[5] Apostle: one sent to do a work, like the twelve disciples of Christ.

[6] Mandarin: a high official of China.

[7] Sedan: a chair with long sticks to be carried by two men.

[8] Queue: it was Chinese custom for men to allow a small area of hair on the back of their head to grow very long, which they braided. This was called a queue.

# CHAPTER ELEVEN

# With the Rev. William Burns

After the retaking of Shanghai by the foreign military forces in February, 1855, I was able to rent a house within the walls of the city. I was very happy to have the chance to live among the crowded population left in the remains of the city that had been destroyed by the war. Here I made my headquarters, being often away on long preaching trips.

On the advice of Rev. Dr. Medhurst, the wise leader of the London Mission, I decided to wear Chinese clothes to make travel and living inland[G] easier. The Chinese had permitted a foreign company to build a silk[1] factory some distance inland. They make the condition that the design of the building must be purely Chinese and that there should be nothing on the outside to show that it was foreign. Much good resulted from this change of clothing. I have continued to wear Chinese clothes as have others in the mission.

Starting in 1851, the Taiping rebellion had reached the limit of its short lived victory. The great city of Nanking had fallen before the attacking army. There, within two hundred miles of Shanghai, the rebels had made their headquarters and begun to strengthen themselves for more victory. During the summer of 1855, many attempts were made to visit the leaders of the rebellion and bring some clear Christian influence upon them. But so little result was seen, these efforts were not continued.

A number of us had tried to reach Nanking. Finding it impossible to do so, I turned my efforts again to spreading the Gospel on the island of Tsungming. Slowly, I was able to overcome the strong feelings against me and the fears of the people. This enabled me to rent a little house and live among them. It was a great joy and made my hope stronger. Sadly, objections were soon made by the local officials to the British Consul,[2] who forced me to leave the area.

At the same time, the French Consul himself had found a property for the Roman Catholic missionaries just a short distance from the house I had to leave. Painfully disappointed by this unexpected problem, I returned to Shanghai, little dreaming of the blessing that God had in store for me there.

The Rev. William Burns of the English Presbyterian Mission, had arrived in that port on his return trip from home. Before going on to his former place of service in the southern province of Fukien, he had tried, like me to visit the Taiping rebels at Nanking. Failing in the attempt, he made his temporary headquarters in Shanghai and worked to evangelise the nearby area that was heavily populated. In the autumn of that year, I was led by God's providing hand to work with this beloved and honoured labourer of God.

We travelled together, spreading the Good News to cities and towns in south Kiangsu and north Chekiang, living in our boats and following the canals[G] and rivers which spread over the whole face of the rich, fertile country. Mr. Burns at that time was wearing English clothes.

He saw that while I was younger and had been in this work a shorter time, I had the quiet listeners while he was followed by the rough fellows. He also saw that I was invited to the homes of the people while he received the excuse that the following crowd was too large. After some weeks, he too began to wear the Chinese clothes and enjoyed the increased acceptance which it gave.

Those happy months were a great joy and almost like a gift to me. His love for the Word was wonderful. His holy, God-honouring life and continual visiting with God made friendship with him satisfying to the deep desire of my heart. His stories of working to spread the Gospel and of mistreatment during his work in Canada, Dublin, and southern China were informative and interesting.

With true spiritual wisdom, he would often point out God's purposes in a way that made the trials of life take on a new outlook and value. He had ideas about evangelism as the great work of the Church. He saw the order of lay evangelists as a lost order that Scripture commands to be put back into use. These thoughts were seeds which were to prove fruitful in the design and planning of the China Inland Mission.

Still, our path was not always a smooth one. When permitted to stay in a city for any length of time, we used the chance completely. After prayer for blessing, we would leave our boats at about nine o'clock in the morning, carrying a light bamboo chair.

Choosing a good place, one of us would stand on the chair and speak for twenty minutes while the other prayed for blessing. Then changing places, the first speaker had a rest. After an hour or two, we would move to distant point and speak again. Usually about noon, we returned to our boats for dinner and prayer and then continued our outdoor work until sunset. After supper and a little rest, we would go with our national helpers to some teashop,[G] where several hours might be spent talking with the people. Many times before leaving a town, we had good reason to believe that much truth had been understood and we placed many Scriptures and books in the hands of those interested.

About this time, the following letter was written by Mr. Burns to his mother at home in Scotland:

> Twenty-five Miles from Shanghai,
> January 26, 1856
>
> Making use of a rainy day which keeps me in my boat, I write a few lines, in addition to a letter to Dundee, containing details which I need not repeat. It is now forty-one days since I left Shanghai on this last trip. A young English missionary, Mr. Taylor, of the Chinese Evangelisation Society,[G] has been my co-worker during these weeks, he in his boat, and I in mine, and we have received much mercy, and at some times, great help in our work.
>
> I must once more tell the story I have had to tell already more than once—how four weeks ago, on December 29, I put on the Chinese clothes, which I am now wearing. Mr. Taylor had made this change a few months before, and I found that because of this he was so much better received by the crowd, that I decided it was my duty to follow his example.
>
> We were at that time more than two times the distance

from Shanghai that we are now, and would still have been at as great a distance had we not met at one place with a group of lawless people, who demanded money and threatened to break our boats if their demands were refused. The boatmen were frightened and made it clear that they wanted to return to some place nearer home. Earlier, these people had violently broken in a part of Mr. Taylor's boat, because their unreasonable demand for books was not obeyed.

We have a large, very large field of labor in this area, while it might be difficult at this time for one to live for very long in any one place; the people listen with thoughtfulness, but we need the power from on High to cause them to understand and be saved. Is there any spirit of prayer for us among God's people in Kilsyth? or is there any effort to seek this spirit? How great the need is, and how great the arguments and reason for prayer in this case. The fruit to be gathered here is very great, and the labourers are few, and imperfectly fitted without much grace for such a work. Yet grace can make the few and weak labourers the means of doing great things—things greater than we can even imagine.

The incident spoken of in this letter took place near the northern border of Chekiang. It led to our return to Shanghai more sooner than we had at first planned. We had reached a busy market town known by the name of Wuchen, or Black Town. We had been told the citizens were the wildest and most lawless people in that part of the country. That was just how we found them to be. The town was a refuge for salt smugglers[G] and many other bad people. The following is taken from my diary[G], written at the time:

January 8, 1856

Started our work in Wuchen this morning by passing out a large number of tracts and some New Testaments. The people seemed very surprised, and we could not learn that any foreigner had been here before. We preached two times; once in the church house of the God of War, and after that in an empty space left by a fire, which had completely destroyed many houses. In the afternoon we preached again to a large group that listened carefully at the same place; and in the evening moved to a teashop[G] where we had a good chance of speaking until many people heard that we were there, and when too many people were coming in, we felt we should leave before our being there slowed the teashop business. Our national helpers, Tsien and Kuei-hua, were able, however, to remain. Returning to our boats, we spoke to a number of people standing on a bridge, and felt we had much reason to be thankful and our hearts were strengthened by the result of our first day's labor.

January 10

First sent Tsien and Kuei-hua to pass out some tracts. After their return we went with them and in a space cleared by fire we separated, and spoke to two groups. On our return to the boats at noon, we found people waiting, as usual, and desiring books. Some were passed out to those who were able to read them. Asking them kindly to excuse us while we ate, I went into my boat and shut the door. Before there was time to pour out a cup of tea a loud noise of something hitting the boat began and the roof was at once broken in. I went out at the back, and found four or five men taking the large pieces of frozen dirt turned up in a field close by— weighing from seven to fourteen pounds (3 to 6 kg.) each— and throwing them at the boat. Reasoning with them was of no use and it was not long before a considerable part of the top part of the boat was broken to pieces, and dirt covered the things inside. Finally, Tsien got a boat that was passing to take him a short distance away, and by passing out a few tracts drew away the thoughts of the men, ending the attack.

We now learned that of those who had done the harm only two were from that place. The others were salt smugglers.[G] The reason was because we had not satisfied their unreasonable demand for books. Through God's providing hand, no one was injured. As soon as it was quiet again, we all met in Mr. Burns's boat and joined in thanksgiving that we had been saved from personal harm, praying also for those who caused the trouble. We prayed that this might be turned to good for us all.

We ate and left the boat, speaking to a large group that soon gathered not far away. We were specially helped by the Lord. Never were we heard with more care. Not one voice was found to side with the men who had troubled us. In the evening the same spirit was shown at the teashops[G] and some seemed to hear with joy the Good News of salvation through a crucified and risen Saviour.

As we came home, we passed a hair cutting shop still open. I went in and while getting my hair cut, spoke to a few people and put two tracts on the wall for others to read.

An honorable shopkeeper by the name of Yao had received parts of the New Testament and a tract, on the first or second day of our stay at Wuchen. He came yesterday when our boat was broken, to beg for some more books. At that time, we were all in disorder from the damage done and from the dirt thrown into the boat. So we asked him to come again in a day or two, when we would be happy to help him. This morning he appeared and handed in the following note:

> On a former day I begged Burns and Taylor, the two "*Rabbis*," to give me good books. It happened at that time those of our town whose hearts were tricked by Satan, not knowing the *Son of David*, were so foolish as to "*raca*" and "*moreh*" and injure your honoured boat. I thank you for promising after this to give the books, and beg the following: Complete New Testament, *Discourse of a Good Man When Near His Death*, *Important Christian Doctrines*, an *Almanac*, *Principles of Christianity*, *Way to Make the World Happy*—of each one copy. Sung and Tsien, and all teachers I hope are well. More praise is unwritten.

This note is interesting, as showing that he had been reading the New Testament thoughtfully, as the italicised words were all taken from it. His use of "raca" and "moreh" for speaking roughly and unkindly, shows their meaning was not lost on him.

After bringing books to this man, we went out with Tsien and Kuei-hua to the east of the town and spoke on the road for a short time. On our return to the boats, I was visited by two Chihli[6] men from the judge's office. The Lord greatly helped me in speaking to them in the Mandarin language of a crucified Saviour. While one of them did not show much concern, the other did and asked questions that showed the interest he was feeling.

When they departed, I left the boat and spoke to the people gathered there, to whom Kuei-hua had been preaching. The setting sun provided an example and reminded one of the words of Jesus, "Night is coming, when no one can work." I spoke of the uncertain length of this life and of the fact that we do not know the time of Christ's return. A degree of deep seriousness settled on them that I had never before seen in China. I began to pray and could see clearly that God was speaking to their hearts. I returned to my boat with a Buddhist[G] priest who had been in the group. He admitted that Buddhism was a system of trickery that could give no hope in death.

January 12

In the afternoon we spoke to the people close to our boats, in one of the roads of the city and in a teashop.[G] Books were passed out each time we spoke. In the evening, we went as usual to speak in the teashops. This time, we decided to go to the opposite end of the town to give the people there a better chance to meet with us. It was a long village, nearly three kilometres in length. As Mr. Burns and I usually talked together in Chinese, this plan was known to those in the boats.

After a short distance, we changed our minds. Instead, we went to the usual teashop, thinking that persons might have gone there expecting to meet us. But this was not the case. We did not find such serious listeners as we had found before. Mr. Burns thought it would be good to leave earlier than usual. We did so, telling Tsien and Kuei-hua that they might remain a little longer.

Returning to the boats, we gave away a few books. It was unusual but we were left to go alone with no one going with us as they usually did. It was no longer a clear night and we found that it had become very dark. On our way we met the boatman who acted as if something were wrong. Without giving any reason, he blew out the light in our lamp. We relighted it, telling him not to put it out again. To our surprise, he carefully put out the light so that it could not be relighted. Then, walking down along a low wall that went out to the river's edge, he looked into the water.

Not knowing what the trouble was, I ran forward to hold him, afraid that he was going to drown himself. I was very thankful when he came quietly back. In answer to our repeated questions, he told us to be very quiet. He said softly that some bad men were wanting to destroy the boats. He and his friends had moved the boats away to escape from them. He then led us to the place where one of the boats was hidden. Before long, Tsien and Kuei-hua came and got safely on the boat. Soon after, we were joined by the teacher Sung and the boat moved away.

The cause of all this trouble was then explained. A man had come to the boats while we were gone, claiming to be a policeman. He carried a written demand for ten dollars[G] and an amount of opium.[G] He said that there were more than fifty country people (salt smugglers[G]) waiting for our answer in a nearby teashop.[G] If we gave them what they wanted and three hundred dollars to pay for their tea, we might remain in peace. But if not, they would come at once and destroy our boats.

Sung told them that we could not obey their demand because our only business was in preaching and passing out books. We had no opium and little money. The man told Sung that he did not believe him. There was nothing for him to do but to ask the man to wait for our return. Not knowing that we had changed our plans, he looked for us in the wrong direction.

While Sung was looking for us, the boatmen had been able to move off. They were very much afraid. Having so recently seen what these men would do openly in the day, they felt no desire to see what they might try by night. When they moved away, they had gone to different places, so that if one boat should be damaged the other might give us an escape. It was after this we had, by God's providing hand, met the boatman and been led onto the boat. As Sung passed the place where the boats had been tied up, he saw twelve or more men between the trees. He heard them asking where the boats had gone but no one could tell. Thankfully, they did not find us.

After some time, the boats joined and moved along together. It was already late. Travelling by night in that part of the country was not the way to escape from evil men. So the question came as to what should be done. This we left for the boatmen to decide. They had moved off of their own decision. We felt that we could not ask others to remain in a position of danger because of us. We strongly asked them to do quickly whatever they planned to do. Tomorrow was the Lord's Day when we did not wish to travel.

We told them that no matter what, we must preach the Gospel. It made little difference where we might stay. Even if we passed the night and were not seen, we were sure to be found out on the following morning. The men decided that we might as well to return to the place from which we had started. This was agreeable to all and so the boatmen turned back. But, they got into another river and pushed along for some time but seemed to have become lost. At last it became very dark, so they tied up the boat for the night.

Calling the boatmen and our national helpers, we read Psalm 91 to them. The words expressed our need at that time. How sweetly cheering was this part of God's Word:

*"1 He who stays under the protection of the Most High will rest in the security of the Almighty. 2 I will say of the LORD, "He is my refuge and my strong house, my God, in whom I trust." 3 Surely he will save you from the one who wants to catch you in his trap and from deadly sickness. 4 He will cover you with his protection, and under his care you will find refuge; his faithfulness will be your defense and safe place. 5 You will not fear the terror of the night, or the arrow that flies by day. . .*
*14 "Because he loves me," says the LORD, "I will rescue him; I will protect him, for he knows my name. 15 He will call upon me, and I will answer him; I will be with him in trouble, I will rescue him and honor him. 16 With long life will I satisfy him and show him my salvation."* (Psalms 91)

With our prayer, we placed ourselves in His care and keeping. He had covered us with thick darkness and permitted us to escape from the hands of vicious men. We retired for the night, thanks to the kind protection of the Watchman of Israel who neither sleeps or forgets His people. We slept in quiet peace and were able to see more clearly, the truth of that Word which I love, "You are my hiding-place and my shield."

Sunday, January 13

This morning I was awakened about 4 a.m. by very sharp pain in the knee-joint. I had hit it so hard the day before that it turned black and blue and now was enlarged and hot. To my great surprise, I heard rain pouring down. The weather had been very nice. On looking out, we found ourselves near the place where we had tied up the boats before. If nothing had happened to stop us, we would have felt it necessary to go into the town to preach as usual. But the rain was so great all day that no one could leave the boats. And so, we enjoyed a very wonderful day of rest, such as we had not had for some time. The weather did not allow much chance for questions to be asked about us. Had the day been fine we would most likely have been discovered, even if we had not left the boats. As it was, we were allowed to think in peace, and with wonder and thankfulness, of the kind dealings of our God, who had in this way led us apart into "a desert place" for a little rest.

Monday, January 14

A cloudless morning. One of the national helpers went before daylight to get some clothes which had been given out for washing. He came back with the news that, even with the pouring rain of yesterday, men had been looking for us in all directions. We had been kept, however, in peace and safety under "the shadow of the Almighty."

The boatmen were now so completely afraid that they would stay no longer and moved off at daylight. I was forced to stay in the boat by my injured knee and had no other choice but to go with them. In the afternoon we reached Pingwang, on the way to Shanghai.

Harm that God blesses is our good,
And unblessed good is harm;
And all is right that seems most wrong,
If it be His sweet will.

[1] Silk: a special kind of cloth.
[2] Consul: a person appointed by his government to live in a foreign city and serve his country's citizens and business interests there.
[3] Canal: like a river, but built by men.
[4] Teashop: a place where tea is served.
[5] Smuggler: one who brings in or takes things out, illegally.
[6] Chihli: this area is in the province of Hopeh in northeast China.
[7] Buddha: the god of a heathen eastern religion.
[8] Opium: a drug that is often misused.

# CHAPTER TWELVE

# Called to Swatow

Leaving the village of Black Town was a real disappointment to us. We had wanted to spend some time there sharing the Gospel. Yet, these trying happenings were a necessary step leading to greater things. God does not permit trials to come without a sure reason. He was leading us by a way that we did not know, but it was His way.

Oh Lord, how happy should we be
If we would throw our care on You,
If we from self would rest;
And feel at heart that One above,
In perfect understanding, perfect love,
Is working for the best!

On arriving in Shanghai, we planned to return in a few days with more books and money. In the city, we met a Christian captain[G] who had been doing business at Swatow. He explained to us what was happening there. There were British people living on Double Island, doing business in drugs and working in the slave trade. Yet, there was no British missionary to preach the Gospel.

The Spirit of God gave me the urge that this was His call. But for days, I felt that I could not obey it. I had never been blessed with such a spiritual father as Mr. Burns and had never known such holy, happy times. I said to myself that it could not be God's will that we should separate.

One evening, I was very troubled and went with Mr. Burns to take tea at the house of the minister, R. Lowrie of the American Presbyterian Mission. He lived at the South Gate of Shanghai. After tea, his wife let us hear "The Missionary Call." Having never heard it before, it had a great effect on me. My heart was almost broken before it was finished. In the words they sang, I said to the Lord:

And I will go.
I may no longer care to give up friends
And my own plans,
And every earthly desire that fastens my heart to you,
my country.

From now on I care not
If storm or sun be my earthly place, bitter or sweet my cup,
I only pray,
God make me holy and my spirit strong for the hard
hour of trouble.

When we left, I asked Mr. Burns to come home with me to the little house that was still headquarters in the city. With much crying, I told him how the Lord had been leading me and that I had been a rebel in not being willing to leave him for this new place. He listened with surprise and happiness and answered that he had, that very night, decided to tell me that he had heard the Lord's call to Swatow. He said that his only sorrow was the thought of leaving me. We went together and began missionary work in that part of China, which in later years has been greatly blessed.

Long before this time, the city of Swatow and the nearby area had been served by the minister, R. Lechler of the Basel Missionary Society.[G] Chased from place to place, he did work that we did not forget and finally retired in Hong Kong. For more than forty years, this minister of God has continued in "great labor." Recently, he has left Hong Kong with his wife, to return again inland and spend the rest of his years among the people he has so long and truly loved.

Captain[G] Bowers was our Christian friend whom God had used to bring the needs of Swatow to Mr. Burns and me. He was full of joy when he heard our decision to give ourselves to preach to this busy, important centre of population. About to sail on his return trip, he offered us free passage on his ship, the *Geelong*. We accepted and left Shanghai early in March, 1856.

A nice trip of six days brought us to Double Island where we found ourselves with a small but very bad group of foreign people. They took part in businesses that included the trade in illegal drugs. We were not willing to be a part of such a group and wanted to live within the city on a part of the mainland seven kilometres away at the mouth of the Han River. We had great difficulty in our attempt to get a place among the people. It seemed as if we should fail and we knew we had to come to the Lord in prayer.

Our God soon did undertake for us. One day, we met with a Cantonese[1] man, a family member of the high official in the town. Mr. Burns spoke to him in the Cantonese language, making him very pleased at being spoken to by a foreign person in his own language. He soon became our friend and rented us a little room in which to stay. We were thankful because it was impossible to find a better place.

Our travels took us around the country. The difficulty and danger was so great that our former work in the North began to appear safe and easy by comparison. The hate and anger of the Cantonese was very painful. We were called "foreign evil spirits," "foreign dog," or "foreign pig." But this led us to walk more closely than ever before with "Him who was not accepted of men."

In our visits to the country, we were in danger of being taken at any time and held for ransom.[2] The people often said that the whole area was "without a king and without law." Certainly, strength was the ruler in those days. At one time, we were visiting a small town and found that the people had captured a wealthy man from another tribe. A large price was asked for his release. Because he refused to pay, they used a stick to cruelly smash the bones just above his feet, one by one. Finally, they received the promise they wanted.

There was nothing but God's protection to keep us from being hurt in the same way. Every town had a wall and would contain ten or twenty thousand people of the same tribe who were often at war with the people living in the next town. To be kindly received in one place was usually a reason for danger in the next. In these times, God's power was often shown.

After a time, the local mandarin[G] became sick and the doctor was unable to help him. Hearing of our medical ministry, he wanted our help. God gave blessing on the medicine given. Thankful for our help, he said we should rent a house for a hospital and a place for people to receive medical treatment. And so, we were able to rent the whole house, one room of which we had lived in before. I had left my medicine and surgery instruments with a friend, the late Mr. Wylie in Shanghai and went back at once to get them.

Mr. Burns came down to see me off from a town called Ampow that we had visited together several times. On my departure, he returned again with two national evangelists sent up from Hong Kong by a minister, J. Johnson, of the American Baptist Missionary Union. The people were willing to listen to their message and accept their books as a gift, but they would not buy them. One night, someone broke in and stole everything they had except their books which were thought to have no value.

Early next morning, people came to buy books. By breakfast, they not only had enough money to buy food, but they also had enough money to pay for one of the men to take a trip to Double Island below Swatow, carrying a letter to Mr. Burns's friend, requesting him to send some of Mr. Burns's money. People came to buy all day and the next day and our friends needed nothing. But on the third day, they could not sell any books. Then, when the money was gone, the messenger returned with more food and things they needed.

Early in July, after about four months' stay in Swatow, I left for Shanghai. I had planned to return in a few weeks with my medical equipment for more work with William Burns. A new field of promise seemed to be opening before us. With much hope, we looked forward to the future. Great blessing was in store for the city and area of Swatow.

But it was not the purpose of God that either of us should remain to experience the result. Soon after I left, Mr. Burns was arrested, put in prison and sent to Canton. On his return to Swatow after war[3] had broken out, he was called away for other service, preventing his future return. On the other hand, my trip to Shanghai proved to be the first step leading to other areas of work.

## THE MISSIONARY CALL

1. My soul is not at rest.
There comes a different and quiet voice to my spirit
Like a dream at night,
That tells me I am on holy ground.

    The voice of my risen Lord, Go teach all nations
    Comes on the night air and awakes my ear.

2. Why do I live here?
The command of God is on me and I may not stop to play with useless things
Or gather earthly flowers,
Until my work is done and my report is given.

3. And I will go.
I may no longer care to give up friends
And my own plans,
And every earthly desire that fastens my heart to you, my country.

4. From now on I care not
If storm or sun be my earthly place, bitter or sweet my cup,
I only pray,
God make me holy and my spirit strong for the hard hour of trouble.

5. And when one for whom
Satan has tried, as he has for me, has received at last
That blessed place
Oh how this heart will shine with thankfulness and love.

    Through all the years of forever my spirit never shall repent
    That work and pain once were mine below.

[1] Canton: old name for the city of Kwangchow.
[2] Ransom: something paid for the release of captured property or persons.
[3] The second war between England and China, which began in 1856.

# CHAPTER THIRTEEN

# Man Proposes, God Will Put In Place

It is interesting to see the different happenings, in the direction of God, which prevented my return to Swatow and led me to settle in Ningpo. This town became the center for me in developing my future work.

On coming to Shanghai to collect the medicine and surgical instruments, my sorrow was great to find that the place had caught fire and everything had been destroyed. This was tragic and I fear I was more like faithless Jacob in believing that everything was against me! For a time, I failed to see that "all things God works for the good of those who love him." I had not then learned to think of God as the Great One in whom "we live, and move and have our being," nor had I come to think of all happenings in life as either directed or permitted by Him. My trial and disappointment was very great.

Medicines cost much in Shanghai, and I had limited money to buy more. I set out on an inland trip to Ningpo, hoping to receive some medicine from Dr. William Parker, who was a member of the same mission as I. With me went the few possessions I had, including my watch, a few surgical instruments, a musical instrument and books for the study of Chinese. I left part of my money behind in Shanghai.

The country was dry for it was the middle of summer and the water level in the canal[G] was very low. Much water had been used for the rice fields while some had been dried up in the great heat. Deciding to make this as much of a mission trip as possible, I set out with many Christian tracts and books. For fourteen days, our crowded boat travelled slowly while I preached and passed out books. We came to a large town called Shihmenwan, where I found that my material had all been given away. I now decided not to go slowly, but to go through the city of Haining, reaching Ningpo as quickly as possible.

August 4, 1856

There was no water beyond Shihmenwan. I paid off my boat and employed two carriers to carry my things as far as Changwan. By the time the sun came up, we were on the way. I walked on alone, leaving my helper to follow with the men who made many stops to rest. On arriving at a city through which we had to pass, I waited for them in a tea shop just outside the North Gate. The carriers arrived slowly and seemed very tired. I soon found that they both smoked opium.[G] They had only carried a load that one strong man would think nothing of taking three times the distance. Yet, they seemed really tired.

After some rice and tea and an hour of rest — and also, I know, a smoke of the pipe — they had a little more energy. I asked them to move on so that we might get to Changwan before the sun became too hot. My helper had a friend in the city, and he wanted to spend the day there and travel on the next morning. I did not like this, but wanted to reach Haining that night if possible.

We set off, entered the North Gate, and had passed through about a third of the city when the carriers stopped to rest and said they should be unable to carry the load on to Changwan. Finally, they agreed to take it to the South Gate, where they were to be paid for the distance they had carried it; and the helper called other carriers to come with them.

Walking ahead, I soon came to Changwan and waited for them to arrive. They seemed to be taking a long time. In the meantime, I asked for more carriers for the rest of the trip to Haining. After some time, I began to wonder at the delay. I was not happy when it became too late to finish the trip to Haining that night. If it were not that my feet hurt and the afternoon very hot, I would have gone back to hurry them on. At last, I decided that my helper must have gone to see his friend and would not come until evening. Yet, even then, there was still no sign of them.

Feeling very troubled, I began very carefully to ask if they had been seen. At last a man asked if I was on a visit from Shihmenwan and going to Haining. He told me that my things had gone on before me. He said that he was sitting in a teashop when a carrier came in and took a cup of tea. Then he set off for Haining in a great hurry, saying that the box and bed were from Shihmenwan and had to be taken to Haining that night. He was to be paid at a rate of ten yuan[G] for each pound." I realised that my things had gone on before me but as it was already dark and I was tired, it was impossible to follow them.

All I could do was to find a place to sleep for the night. This was not an easy task. Raising my heart to God in prayer and asking for help, I went to the other end of town, hoping that the news of a foreign person in town might not have spread this far. I soon came to a small country hotel and went in. In the dark, I hoped to pass without any question. The only food they had was cold rice and snakes cooked in lamp oil. Not wanting to be asked about my nationality, I thought it wise to order and eat. The food was not to my liking.

I asked the owner if I could spend the night. He produced a record book, advising me that in these difficult times, they were ordered by the officials to keep a record of the people who stay. He asked for my honorable family name. I told him that my unworthy family name was Tai.

"And your honorable second name?"

"My unworthy name is Ia-Koh" (James).

He told me that it was an unusual name that he had never heard before. He asked me how I wrote it. I added that it was a common name in the place from which I had come."

"And may I ask from where you come and where you are going?"

"I am going from Shanghai to Ningpo, by way of Hangchow."

Then, he asked what kind of work I did. I told him that I cure the sick. "Oh! you are a doctor," the owner said. To my great satisfaction, he closed the book. His wife continued talking with me.

"You are a doctor, are you?" she said; "I am happy about that, for I have a daughter who is sick with a terrible disease. If you will cure her, you shall have your supper and bed for nothing." I asked what my supper and bed were to cost and found they were less than three halfpence of our money! The girl had leprosy[2] for which I had no medicine. Unable to help the girl, I would not tell her what she needed, saying that her disease was one that was difficult to get over and that I had no way of helping her.

The mother brought a pen and paper, asking that I write what she needed. She said, this would do no harm, even if it does no good. But this also I would not do. I asked to be shown my bed. Led to a very terrible room on the ground floor, I passed the night without bed or anything except my shoes to place my head on. There was no protection from insects. Ten or eleven other people were sleeping in the same room, so I could not take anything off, for fear that someone might steal. As the night went on, I became very cold.

August 5

As may be expected, I rose with little rest and felt very far from well. It was a long time before breakfast was ready. There was another delay before I could get change for the only piece of money I had with me. I did not receive the full value for this coin, which was a serious loss to me in my trying position.

I looked through the town for news of my helper and carriers but found nothing. It was possible that they had arrived later or come on in the morning. The town was large and nearly three kilometres long. Because of tiredness and pain, I set out for Haining in the full heat of the day. The trip of about thirteen kilometres, took a long time but I was able to find a welcome place to rest and cup of tea at a village halfway along the road. A strong rain came, allowing me time to preach a little to the people.

It was almost sundown when I arrived at the north area of Haining. When I asked there, I heard no news and was told that outside the East Gate, I should be more likely to hear of them. But I did not find them. While sitting in a tea shop to rest, a number of people from the mandarin's office asked who I was and where I had come from. On learning the object of my search, one of the men told me that a box and a bed were carried past here about half an hour ago.

The carrier seemed to be going towards either the Great East Gate or the South Gate. He advised me to go to the business houses there and ask. I asked him to go with me but he would not come, even though I offered to pay. Another man offered to go with me, so we set off together. We searched both inside and outside the two gates but with no result. I asked a man to make a careful search, promising extra pay if he should find them. In the meantime, I had some dinner and preached to a group of people who had gathered.

He returned, having found nothing. By now very tired, I asked him to help me find a place to sleep for the night and then I would pay him for his trouble. We set off in search of a place to sleep. At the first two resting houses, the people appeared willing for us to stay but later changed their minds. A government officer who followed us seemed to cause them concern. We went to a third house and found a place to stay. We were no longer followed by the government worker. Some tea was brought and I paid the man for his trouble.

Soon after he was gone, some government officials came but went away. I was now told I could not stay for the night. A young man blamed the officials for the unkindness and told me not to worry. He invited me to sleep at his house. I went with him, but the family were not willing to receive me. Being tired, I found it difficult to stand, but had again to seek a place to stay. Then they said, because a crowd had gathered at the door, they wanted me to wait at a nearby tea shop until the people went away. Then I could return to the house.

Having no other choice, I left with the young man and waited until past the middle of the night. On returning to the house, the young man searched but could not find it. I was led to another part of the city where he finally left me to pass the rest of the night as best I could.

I was opposite a place of worship but it was closed, so I lay down on the stone steps in front. Putting my money under my head, I would soon have been asleep if I had not sensed a person coming towards me. He was a beggar, so common in China. I knew that he wanted to rob me of my money. I lay watching his every move. I also looked to my Father not to leave me in this hour of trial. The man came up and examined me for some time to be sure that I was sleeping. It was so dark that he could not see my eyes fixed on him. As he began to feel about me, I quietly asked what he wanted. He made no answer, but went away.

I was very thankful to see him go. Putting as much of my money as I could into my pocket, I hid the rest in another part of my clothes. I made a place to rest near the wall and soon began to go to sleep, but I was awakened by the quiet steps of two people coming. My body was so tired that any little noise caused me to awake. Again I asked for protection from Him who alone was my help. I lay still as before.

One of them began to feel for the money under my head. I spoke again. They sat down at my feet, telling me that they planned to stay there. I asked that they take the opposite side as there was plenty of room. I wanted them to leave this side to me, but they would not move from my feet. I raised myself and set my back against the wall.

They said I had better lie down and sleep as I would be unable to walk tomorrow. They told me that I should not be afraid as they would protect me for the rest of the night. I spoke firmly to them that I did not want their protection, nor did I need it. I told them that I was not Chinese and did not worship their god who does not give any help. I worshiped God who is my trusted Father. I told them directly that I knew well what they were and what they wanted to do. I would be keeping my eye on them and would not sleep.

One of them went away, but soon returned with a third person. I had no feeling of ease, but looked to God for help. Now and then, one of them would get up to see if I were sleeping. I told him not to be mistaken as I was awake. Sometimes, my head would fall and this would be a signal for one of them to rise. At once, I woke up and said something. As the night passed slowly on, I felt very tired. To keep myself awake and to cheer myself, I sang songs, said Scripture and prayed in English. These people would have given anything for me to stop, but gave me no more trouble. Shortly, before the sun rose, they left and I was able to sleep.

August 6

I was awakened by the young man who had troubled me the evening before. He was not very gentle and kept asking for me to pay him for his work. He even tried to force me to do what he wanted. I defended myself quickly without any thought and took hold of his arm with unexpected strength and told him not to lay a finger on me again or get in my way. This really caused him to change. He let me quietly remain until the gun announced the opening of the gates of the city and then begged for money to buy opium.[G] I refused but gave him only the price of fuel that he said he had used in my company the night before. I later learned that he was connected with one of the government offices.

As soon as possible, I bought rice and tea for breakfast and made another search for my things but found nothing. I set out on the return trip and after a long, tiring and painful walk, arrived in Changwan about noon. I failed to find any of my lost things. I had some food in a tea shop, washed myself and slept until four in the afternoon.

Feeling much better, I set off to return to the South Gate of the city where I had left my helper and carriers two days before. On the way, I was led to think about the goodness of God. I remembered that I had not yet prayed that I might have a place to stay that night. I felt ashamed that I had been so concerned for my few things while many unsaved people around me had caused so little emotion. I came as a sinner and asked for forgiveness through the blood of Jesus, knowing that I was accepted in Him — free, clean, sanctified.

Oh, the love of Jesus, how great I felt it to be! I knew more than I had ever before, what it was to be turned away from and not be accepted. I was like one from whom men hid their faces with nowhere to lay my head. I felt more than ever before, the greatness of that love which caused Him to leave His home in glory and suffer this for me, even to lay down His life upon the cross. I thought of Him as "turned away from and not accepted of men, a man of great sorrow, and One who knew sorrow." I thought of Him at Jacob's well, tired, hungry, and needing something to drink, yet He found His meat and drink in doing His Father's will.

I had to compare this with my little love. I looked to Him for pardon for the past and grace and strength to do His will in the future. I needed to walk much more closely in His steps and more than ever to be completely His. I prayed for myself, for friends in

England and for my brothers in the work. To my eyes came such sweet tears of joy mixed with sorrow. The tiredness from the road was almost forgotten. Before I knew it, I had arrived at the city. At the South Gate, I took a cup of tea, asked about my lost things and spoke of the love of Jesus. Then I entered the city. Receiving no help with my question, I left by the North Gate.

I felt so much better both in mind and body because of my talk with the Lord on the road back to the city. I decided I would be able to finish the other six miles back to Shihmenwan that evening. First, I went in to another tea shop to buy food where I met one of the same carriers who had earlier carried my things. I learned that after I had left them, they had taken my things to the South Gate. There my helper told them that I had gone on, that he did not want to start at once, but would spend the day with his friend and come back to me.

They carried the things to his friends house and left them there. I asked him to go with me to the house and learned that my helper had spent the day and night with them. The next morning, he had called other carriers and set off for Hangchow. This was all I could learn. Unable to do anything but return to Shanghai, I left the city again. It was now too late to go to Shihmenwan. I looked to my Father to provide all my needs and again I was reminded of His unending love and care. I was invited to sleep on a passenger boat, now dry in the bed of the river. The night was again very cold and insects troublesome. Still, I got a little rest. When the sun came up, I continued my trip.

August 7

I felt very sick at first. Yet, I reminded myself of the goodness of God so that I could stand the heat each day and the long cold at night. Much of the load was taken off my mind. I had given myself and my cares to the Lord and knew that if it was for my good and for His glory, my things would be returned. If not, all would be for the best. I hoped that the most difficult part of my trip was now coming to a close. As I walked, I was still tired and my feet hurt.

On my return to Shihmenwan, I still had 810 yuan[G] in hand. The cost to take the boat to Kashing was 120 yuan with the trip to Shanghai costing 360, leaving me just 330 yuan for three or four days' needs. I went at once to the boat office. To my disappointment I found that because the river was dry, the shipment had not come down. No boat would leave that day and perhaps not even the next. I asked if there was not a letter-boat for Kashing and was told that these had already left. All I could do was to travel with any private boat that was going. I could find no boat that was going all the way to Shanghai. If I had, my difficulty would have been at an end.

Just at this time I saw at a turn in the river, a letter-boat going in the direction of Kashing. This must have been one of the Kashing boats that had an unexpected delay. I set off as fast as I could possibly go. I forgot about my tired body and feet that hurt. After a chase of about two kilometres, I caught up with it.

"Are you going to Kashing?" I called out.

"No," was the only answer.

"Are you going in that direction?"

"No."

"Will you let me go as far as you do go that way?"

Still, "No," and nothing more.

Completely disappointed and my strength gone, I fell to the grass and fell into a deep sleep, as if dead. On waking, I heard voices coming to my ears. They were talking about me! One said, "He speaks the pure Shanghai language." From their own language, I knew them to be Shanghai people. Raising myself, I saw that they were on a large passenger boat on the other side of the river. After a few words, they sent their small boat to get me. They were very kind and gave me some tea. When I felt better, I was given food also.

I removed my shoes to ease my feet and I was kindly given hot water to wash. On hearing my story and seeing how bad my feet looked, they felt sorry for me. Every passing boat was stopped to see if it was going my way. They did not find one, so after a few hours' sleep, I left the boat planning to preach in the house of worship of Kwan-ti.

I had told my new friends that I was now unable to help myself, having no strength to walk to Kashing. Unable to get a ride that day, I no longer had enough money to take me by letter-boat, a costly way to travel. I said that I did not know how my God would help me, but that I knew He would do so. My business was now to serve Him where I was. I knew that help would come and said that this would prove the truth of that which other missionaries and I had preached at Shanghai.

While visiting with the captain[G] on the way to town, we saw a letter boat coming up. I reminded him that I no longer had the money to pay my passage. However, he stopped it and found that it was going to a place about fifteen kilometres from Shanghai. From there, one of the boat men would carry the mail over land to the city. He informed them that I was a foreigner from Shanghai with no money to go back. He told them that if they would take me with them and find a sedan[G] chair for the rest of the way, I would pay them in Shanghai.

The captain pointed to his boat sitting on the mud because of the low level of water. He promised that if I did not pay on my return to Shanghai, he would do so on their return. This kindness was not asked for and made by someone I did not know. This was unusual as Chinese people generally do not take chances with their money. Those on the letter-boat agreed to this and I was taken on as a passenger. Oh, how thankful I felt for this guidance of God and to be once more on my way to Shanghai!

This boat was built long and thin and did not have very much space inside. One has to lie down all the time as any small move would easily cause the boat to turn over. This did not concern me, as I was only too happy to be quiet. These are the fastest boats I have seen in China and worked by two men who take turns all day and night. They use their feet and hands. If the wind is right, they work their feet and use one hand to control a small sail, guiding with the other hand.

After a nice and quick trip, I arrived safely in Shanghai on August 9, through the help of Him who has said, "Never will I leave you. Never will I forsake you." He also promised "And surely I am with you always, to the very end of the age."

[1] Yuan: the money of China.

[2] Leprosy: a very serious sickness that effects the skin, flesh, and nerves. It deforms and wastes body parts.

CHAPTER FOURTEEN

# Divine Guidance

It now seemed very clear that the lost property had been stolen by my helper who had gone off with it to Hangchow. Included was everything I had in China, except for a small amount of money left in Shanghai. The first question was how best to act for the good of the man who had been the cause of so much trouble. It would not have been difficult to take steps that would have led to his punishment. Still, the chance of being repaid for the loss was very small. But my main concern was that the thief[G] was a man for whose salvation I had worked and prayed. I felt that to have him punished would not be a witness to the teaching of Jesus, of which we had read together, “But I tell you, do not resist an evil person.”

Finally, I decided that his soul was of more value than the things I had lost. I wrote and told him this, trying to show him the need to repent and have faith in the Lord Jesus Christ. The way I did this made my Christian friends in England thankful, one of whom was later led to send me money to replace the amount I lost. This was the first of more money received from the same kind helper. He was Mr. George Mueller of Bristol.

After I collected the little money left in Shanghai, I set out again for Ningpo to seek help from Dr. Parker in replacing the medicine I had lost by fire. When this was done, I returned to Shanghai, hoping to soon be working with my friend, Mr. Burns, in Swatow. Yet, God had a different plan and the delay caused by the robbery was just enough to keep me from starting for the South as I had wanted to do.

The government politics was not certain and there was danger of coming war. Early in October of this year (1856) there began a most hostile situation. Very soon China was to be deeply involved in a second long hostile situation with foreign powerful nations. All missionary work had to stop for a while, especially in the South. News of these happenings and letters from Mr. Burns, arrived just in time to meet me in Shanghai as I was leaving for

Swatow. Since I was prevented from going, I could clearly see that the hand of God closed the door I had so much wanted to enter.

While in Ningpo, I got to know Mr. John Jones. He, along with Dr. Parker were with the Chinese Evangelisation Society[G] in that city. Unable to return to Swatow, I decided to join these brothers in the Lord in their Ningpo work. I set out at once. On the afternoon of the second day, about thirty-five kilometres from Shanghai, Mr. Jones and I came near the large and important city of Sungkiang. I spoke of going to preach the Gospel to the many people who lived along the edge of the river and crowded the road to the city gates.

Among the passengers on the boat was one intelligent man who had been involved in much travel and been to other nations. He had even visited England where he went by the name of Peter. As might be expected, he had heard something of the Gospel, but did not have a personal experience of its saving power. On the evening before, I had spoken to him about his salvation. The man was willing to listen and even moved to cry, but still he was not saved. I was pleased when he asked to go with me and hear me preach.

I went into the cabin[G] of the boat to prepare tracts and books to give away with my Chinese friend, when I was startled by a fall and a cry from outside. Springing to the floor of the boat, I took a quick look at the situation. Peter was gone! The other men were all there on the boat, looking at the place where he had disappeared but made no effort to save him. A strong wind was taking the boat quickly forward although there was a strong current in the opposite direction. The land close by gave us no way of telling how far we had left the man who had fallen into the water.

I quickly let down the sail and jumped into the water in hope of finding him. I looked around in frightened terror and saw a small fishing boat nearby. "Come!" I said in a loud voice, as hope came into my heart. "Come over here; a man in the water is about to die right here!"

"Veh bin" was the answer. This meant that it was not a good time.

"Do not talk like that!" I said; "a man is about to die in this water, I tell you!"

"We are busy fishing," they said, "and cannot come."

"Never mind trying to catch fish," I said, "I will give you more money than many trying to catch fish today will bring home; only come—come at once!"

"How much money will you give us?"

"We cannot wait to discuss that now! Come, or it will be too late. I will give you five dollars[G]."

"We will not do it for that," said the men. "Give us twenty dollars and we will try to rescue him."

"I do not have that much. Do come quickly and I will give you all I have!"

"How much may that be?"

"I don't know exactly, about fourteen dollars."

At last, the boat was slowly brought over and they worked to get the man out of the water. It took less than a minute to pull his body into the boat. The men were angry. They did not receive their money quickly because we were trying to help the man breath again. But all was lost. He had drowned.

This incident was very sad to me and full of meaning. It taught a far more terrible warning. Were not those men in the boat guilty of this poor man's death? They had the means to rescue him but refused to do it. And yet, let us not judge against them, because a greater than Nathan might answer, "You are the man." Is it so evil a thing to refuse to save the body? How much worse will be the punishment of one who would leave the soul to die, saying "Am I my brother's keeper?"

The Lord Jesus gave a command to you and me to go into all the world and preach the Gospel to every person. Shall we tell him that it is not a good time to do this? Shall we tell Him that we are busy at our work and cannot go? Shall we say we have bought an animal or have a husband or wife? Perhaps we are involved in other and more interesting things and cannot go.

Before long "we must all appear before the judgment seat of Christ, that each one may receive what is due to him for the things done while in the body, whether good or bad." Let us remember.

Let us pray for and labor for the unsaved Chinese. Or we shall sin against our own soul. Let us consider who it is that has said, "Rescue those being led away to death. Hold back those staggering towards slaughter. If you say, 'But we knew nothing about this,' does not He who weighs the heart perceive it? Does not he who guards your life know it? Will he not repay each person according to what he has done?" (Proverbs 24.11-12)

Through the darkness of the night in Macedon,[3]
The cry of many as of one;
The silence of no hope
Is given in terrible prayer!
The soul's great bitter cry,
"Come over and help us, or we die."

How with sorrow it keeps on,
For half the earth is Macedon;
These brothers to their brothers call,
And by the Love which loves them all,
And by the whole earth's Life they cry,
"Oh you that live, look, we die!"

By other noise the world is won
Than that which calls from Macedon;
The loud sound of gain around it rolls,
Or man to himself will sell
And cannot listen to the foreign cry
"Oh hear and help us, or we die!"

Yet with that cry from Macedon
The cause of Christ rolls on:
"I come; who would live in My day,
In another area prepare My way;
My voice is crying in their cry,
Help you the dying, or you will die."

Jesus, for men of Man the Son,
Yes, Your cry from Macedon;
Oh, by the kingdom[G] and the power
And glory of Your coming hour,
Awake heart and will to hear their cry;
Help us to help them, or we die.

[1] Thief: a person who steals in a secret way.
[2] Cabin: a small house or room.
[3] Macedon: a place in the Bible that needed missionary help.
[4] Kingdom: the country of a king, used here as the place where God's will is done.

CHAPTER FIFTEEN

# Living in Ningpo

The autumn of 1856 was well gone before I got to Ningpo, a very ancient and important city on the coast of China. Opened by the treaty[1] of Nanking in 1842, to enable foreign people to live there, it had long been the place of missionary work. The many streets are full of life. Four hundred thousand people live within or around the eight kilometre area of its ancient wall, every one a soul that Jesus loves and for whom He died.

As winter came, I rented a house in Wu-gyiao-deo or Lake Head Street. It was not a nice place in which to live. I clearly remember writing the first letter of my name in the snow which fell on my bed in the large upstairs room. This room was now divided into four or five smaller separate rooms. The roof of a Chinese house may keep off the rain but it does not give good protection against snow which will blow up through any small opening in the wall and find its way inside. Although it was not completely finished, the little house made a nice place to stay during my time of work among the people. There I thankfully lived and found plenty of ways to serve —morning, noon and night.

During the last part of this year, my mind was greatly concerned about continuing to work with my mission because it was often in debt.[G] I had always stayed away from debt and kept within my salary,[G] although at times only by being very careful. Now there was no difficulty in doing this, for my income was larger. Because the country was at peace, things did not cost as much.

But the society[G] itself was in debt. My fellow missionaries and I were told to draw money for our salaries. But, the society often had to borrow to pay us. I finally decided in the following year to stop my work with the society because my heart was troubled by this problem.

The teaching of God's Word seemed unmistakably clear: *"Owe no man anything."*(KJV) To my mind, borrowing money means a conflict of Scripture — a belief that God has not given some good thing and we decide to get this for ourselves. Could that which was wrong for one Christian be right for a group of Christians? Or could any number of mistakes we made before make it right to do it now? If the Word taught me anything, it was to have no connection with debt.

I could not think that God was poor, that He was short of what we need or not willing to provide for whatever work was truly His. It seemed that if there were any lack of money to carry on work, in that project or at that time, it could not be the work that God wanted done. To satisfy my conscience, I resigned from the society which had given me my salary.

I was happy that my friend and fellow worker, Mr. Jones, was also led to leave the society for the same reason. We were both thankful that we left without any break in friendship or cross words on either side. We had the joy of knowing our feeling was shared by several people on the committee although the society as a whole, could not come to our position. We trusted God alone for what we needed and were able to continue a connection with the people who cared for us. We sent home reports for publication as before as long as the society continued to exist.

This step was more than a little trying to our faith. I was not at all sure of what God would have me do, or if He would meet my needs so that I could continue working as before. I had no friends from whom I expected help. I did not know what means the Lord might use, but was willing to give up all my time to the service of evangelisation among the unsaved. I would be pleased if He would give me any small amount on which I could live.

If He were not pleased with this, I was prepared to do whatever work might be necessary to help myself. I would give as much time as possible to more missionary efforts. But God gave His blessing and help. How happy and thankful I felt when I was able to leave! I could look right up into my Father's face with a satisfied heart, ready by His grace, to follow Him. I felt very sure of His loving care.

With what blessing He did lead me and provide for me I can never, never tell. It was like some of my early home experiences. My faith was not without trial and often failed. I was so sorry and ashamed that I failed to trust such a Father. But oh, I was learning to know Him! I would not even then have chosen to be without the trial. He became so near, so real, so close to me.

Once in a while, money was short. It was not because I did not have enough for personal needs but because I gave help to the needy and dying people around me. There were many trials that went beyond these, causing me to look deep into my heart, and being deeper, brought much more rich fruit. How happy I am to know that what Miss Havergal said is true.

"They who trust Him completely, find Him completely true."

I have learned that when we fail to trust fully, He still remains faithful and does not change. He is completely true even if we trust or not. *"If we are faithless, he will remain faithful, for he cannot disown himself."* (2 Timothy 2:13) But oh, how we do not please our Lord whenever we fail to trust Him. What peace, blessing, and victory we lose when we sin against the faithful One! May we never again refuse to trust Him!

The year 1857 was a time of trouble. At the end of that year, there was an attack on Canton by the British. This marked the beginning of England's second Chinese war. Talk of trouble was everywhere. In many places, the missionaries passed through much danger. In Ningpo, we faced a considerable threat to our lives, but God took care of us in answer to prayer.

The attack of Canton began. When the news came to the Cantonese in Ningpo, they were very angry. They immediately set to work to destroy all the foreign people living in the city. It was well known that many of the foreigners used to meet for worship every Sunday evening at the house of a missionary. The plan was to encircle the place at a certain time and kill all foreigners present. Then they would kill any who were not at the meeting.

The Tao-t'ai, or chief official of the city, easily agreed to this plan. The plan was now ready to be carried out and the foreigners knew nothing about what was to happen. A similar plot against the Portuguese people was carried out a few months later and between fifty and sixty were killed in open daylight. It so happened, one of those who knew about the plot had a friend who worked for the missionaries and wanted them to be safe. He was led to warn his friend of the coming danger and advise him to stop working for foreigners. The helper made this known to the missionary for whom he worked. The little group then knew about their danger. On realising how serious the situation was, they decided to meet at one of the missionary houses and hide under the protection of God's care. They did this with good results.

At the very time we were praying to the Lord, he led a lower public official, the Superintendent[4] of Customs, to call upon the Tao-t'ai and argue with him on the matter. He told him that any such thing would cause the foreigners in other places to come with an army to fight them and destroy the city. The Tao-t'ai said that when the foreigners came, he should deny knowing anything of the plot and direct their anger against the Cantonese who would then be destroyed. He planned to destroy both Cantonese and foreigners by one trick.

The Superintendent of Customs let him know that all such attempts to escape punishment would not work. Finally, the Tao-t'ai sent a message to the Cantonese, removing his approval of the attack. This took place at the very time when we were asking protection of the Lord, although we did not know about this until some weeks later. Here again, we were led to prove that "His arm alone, is enough and our protection is sure."

I cannot attempt to give any history of what happened during this time. When 1857 came to an end, Mr. Jones and I had the joy of many blessings. It is interesting to remember the happenings connected with the first confession of faith in Christ, which brought us new hope.

At one time I was preaching the good news of salvation through the finished work of Christ, when a man of middle age stood up and gave witness of his salvation and his faith in the power of the Gospel.

"I have long looked for the truth," he said, "as my fathers did before me, but I have never found it. I have been far and near, but without having it. I have found no rest in Confucianism,[G] Buddhism[G], or Taoism;[G] but I do find rest in what I have heard here tonight. From now on, I am a believer in Jesus."

This man was a leading official of a group of Buddhists in Ningpo. A short time after his confession of faith, there was a meeting of the group for which he had at one time been responsible. I went with him to that meeting. To the ones who once worshiped with him, he told about the peace he had received in believing. Soon after this, one of his friends was saved and baptised. Both are now in heaven. The first of these two continued to preach the good news of great joy. A few nights after he was saved, he asked how long this Gospel had been known in England. We told him we had known it for hundreds of years.

"What!" said he, surprised. "Is it possible that for hundreds of years, you have the known about the good news and have only now come to preach it to us? My father looked for the truth for more than twenty years and died without having it. Oh, why did you not come sooner?"

Many people have died since that sad question was asked. But how many might repeat the same question today? More than two hundred million since then have gone into eternity without the hope of salvation. How long shall this continue and the words of Jesus, "to every person," go without being obeyed?

[1] Treaty: an agreement.
[2] Debt: to owe money to others.
[3] Salary: money received for working.
[4] Superintendent: one who is in charge.
[5] Confucianism: a heathen eastern religion.
[6] Taoism: a heathen eastern religion.

CHAPTER SIXTEEN

# Having What We Need On Time

Very often our God brings His people into trials so that they may come to know Him as they could not otherwise do. He will then show Himself as "an ever-present help in trouble" and make the heart happy each time He shows His faithfulness. We who only see such a small part of our trials, often feel that we would not want to miss them. How much more shall we want to bless and worship His name when all the things we cannot see are brought to light!

In the autumn of 1857, just one year after I came to settle in Ningpo, a little incident happened that did much to strengthen our faith in the loving and kind God and His all seeing care. A brother in the Lord, the Rev. John Quarterman, of the American Presbyterian Mission North, was taken with severe smallpox.[1] My sad duty was to take care of him until his death. Then it became necessary to do away with the clothing worn while taking care of him, for fear of giving the disease to others.

Not having enough money in hand to purchase what was needed, prayer was the only answer. The Lord answered it by the unexpected coming of a long-lost box of clothing from Swatow that had remained in the care of the Rev. William Burns when I left him in Shanghai in the early summer of the year before. These things came at the right time and brought a sweet sense of the Father's own care to provide them. About two months later the following was written:

November 18, 1857

Many seem to think that I am very poor. This certainly is true enough in one sense, but I thank God it is "poor, yet making many rich; having nothing, and yet possessing everything." And my God shall give everything I need; to Him be all the glory. I would not, if I could, live in a different way than I am —completely dependent upon the Lord, and used as an instrument to help others.

On Saturday, November 4, our home mail arrived. That morning we gave the usual breakfast to about seventy of the very poor. Sometimes, there are fewer than forty while at other times, more than eighty. They come to us every day, except for the Lord's Day. On that day we are unable to feed them and get through our other work as well.

On that Saturday morning, we paid all that we owed and made sure we had enough food for ourselves for the next day. After this, there was no money left between us. How the Lord was going to provide for Monday we knew not. Over our fireplace, there were two written messages in Chinese letters — Ebenezer, "Thus far has the LORD helped us." and Jehovah-Jireh, "The Lord will provide" — and He kept us from doubting for a time.

That very day the mail came in, a week sooner than was expected. Mr. Jones received a bank check for $214. We gave God thanks and took new strength. The check was taken to a storekeeper. There was usually a delay of several days to get the money. This time, he said, "Send down on Monday." Although he had not been able to exchange all the dollars[G], he let us have seventy. So all was well. Oh, it is sweet to live in this way and depend upon the Lord who never will fail us!

On Monday, the poor had their breakfast as usual. We had not told them not to come, knowing that the Lord would provide for His work. We could not keep our eyes from filling with tears of thankfulness when we saw not only our own needs met, but those of the widow[2] and the orphan,[3] the blind and the lame.[4] The friendless and the poor, together had their needs met by Him who is able to feed the birds.

*"Glorify the LORD with me: let us lift and honor his name together. Taste and see that the LORD is good; blessed is the man who takes refuge in him. Fear the Lord, you his saints,[5] for those who fear him lack nothing. The lions[6] may grow weak and hungry but those who seek the LORD lack no good thing."* If a thing is not good, why would we want it?

But even $200 cannot last forever. By New Year's Day, we did not have much again. At last, on January 6, 1858, only one coin remained — 1/20 of a penny[G] — in the joint possession of

Mr. Jones and me. We looked to God once again to show His kind care. Enough food was found in the house for a small breakfast. After that, we could only take ourselves to Him who was able to give us all that we need with the request, "Give us this day our daily bread." We had no food in the house nor money to buy any.

After prayer and much thought, we decided that we should try to sell something in order to meet our immediate needs. On looking around, we saw nothing that we could sell and little that the Chinese would purchase for ready money. We could have borrowed but this we felt was not in agreement with Scripture. We had one thing — an iron stove[7] which we knew the Chinese would buy quickly. But we did not want to sell.

A while later, we set out to the founder's,[8] and after a walk of some distance came to the river which we had wanted to cross by a floating bridge of boats. Here the Lord blocked our path. The bridge had been carried away the night before and we could only cross the river by boat, the payment for which was two coins for each person. As we only possessed one coin, we had to return and wait on His plan for us.

On arriving at home, we found that Mrs. Jones had gone by invitation with the children to eat at a friend's house. Mr. Jones had been invited but refused to go and leave me with nothing to eat. We carefully looked through the cupboards.[9] Though there was nothing to eat, we found a small amount of cocoa,[10] which we drank with a little hot water. After this, we prayed to the Lord who heard and saved us. While we were still upon our knees, a letter arrived from England containing a payment to us.

This not only met the immediate and urgent need of that day but some future needs as well, for I was to marry just fourteen days after this date. I was strengthened in my sure belief that God would not allow shame to come to those whose complete and only trust was in Him. There was no disappointment for "Though the mountains be shaken and the hills be removed, yet my unfailing love for you will not be shaken nor my covenant[11] of peace be removed," says the LORD. During the following years, our faith was often greatly tested. Yet, He always proved faithful to His promise and never allowed us to lack any good thing.

Never were there two people to marry who more fully knew the truth, *"He who finds a wife finds what is good and receives blessing from the LORD."* (Proverbs 18:22) My beloved wife was not only a great gift to me. God made her a great blessing during the twelve years she was given to China and to the many people who loved her.

She had a life long connection with missionary work in that great land. Her father, the beloved and faithful Samuel Dyer, was among the first missionaries of the London Mission in the East. He arrived at the Straits Settlements on the southwest coast of the Malay Peninsula as early as 1827 and for sixteen years, worked hard among the Chinese in Penang and Singapore, finishing a valuable font[12] of Chinese metal type,[13] the first of the kind that had been made.

Dying in 1843, Mr. Dyer was never able to see his hopes of finally settling in China. But his children lived to see the country opened to the Gospel and to take their share in the great work that had been so close to his heart. Before we were to marry, my beloved wife had been already living in Ningpo for several years with her friend, Miss Aldersey and was well able to give valuable help to her.

[1] Smallpox: a disease that will affect the skin.
[2] Widow: a woman whose husband is dead.
[3] Orphan: a child whose parents are dead.
[4] Lame: a person who cannot walk.
[5] Saint: another name for a Christian.
[6] Lion: a large wild cat.
[7] Stove: burns fuel or uses electricity to provide heat to cook.
[8] Founder: one who works with melted metal.
[9] Cupboard: a place where food is kept.
[10] Cocoa: a seed which is ground up and used to make a drink or food.
[11] Covenant: an agreement.
[12] Font: a group or set of letters all of one size used in printing or writing.
[13] Type: a letter or number.

CHAPTER SEVENTEEN

# God a Refuge for Us

In 1859, I experienced a somewhat different but no less real answer to prayer. My beloved wife was brought very low with sickness. At last, all hope of getting better was gone. Every treatment proved to be useless. Dr. Parker had nothing more to offer. Her life was going away fast. The only hope was that God might yet raise her up, in answer to believing prayer.

There was the usual afternoon prayer meeting among the missionaries and I sent in a request for prayer. At this time, an untried treatment came to my mind. I felt that I must hurry to talk with Dr. Parker to seek his opinion. This was a time of extreme sorrow. The drawn look about her face and eyes showed the time of death was near. There was a question of her life holding out until my return.

It was nearly two miles to Dr. Parker's house and it appeared to be a long way. On my way, I tried to seek God in prayer. The great words were brought with power to my soul, "Call upon me in the day of trouble. I will deliver you and you will honour me." I was at once able to claim them in faith and the result was deep, unspeakable peace and joy.

All thinking about distance was gone. Dr. Parker approved of the treatment I was thinking of. But on coming home, I saw that the needed change had taken place with neither this treatment nor any other. The drawn look of her face had changed to the calmness of quiet sleep. No mark of sickness remained to slow her getting well.

Since my own loved one had not seen death, it was with added sympathy and sorrow that I felt for Dr. Parker. In the autumn of the same year, his own wife was taken very quickly. It was necessary for the doctor to return to Glasgow at once with his children who now had no mother. A temporary plan had to be made for the work of the Mission hospital in Ningpo, for which he alone had been responsible. He asked me to take over the work, especially the dispensary.[1] After a few days of waiting upon the Lord for guidance, I felt led to take not only the dispensary work, but also the hospital. I trusted the faithfulness of a God who hears and answers prayer to provide the means needed for the work.

Up to this time, the money for taking care of the hospital had been provided by the doctor's medical care to foreigners. When he left, this money stopped coming in. But had not God said that whatever we ask in the name of the Lord Jesus shall be done? Are we not told to seek first the kingdom[G] of God, not ways to make it go forward and that all these things shall be added to us? Such promises were enough. Eight days before taking this work, I had no idea of ever doing so. Even less could friends at home have thought I would do it. But the Lord had seen the need before and already money was on the way to meet the need.

At times, there were no less than fifty sick people in the hospital, along with a large number who came for treatment but didn't need to stay in the hospital. Thirty beds were usually given free to sick people and their nurses. About as many were given to opium[G] smokers who paid for their stay while having treatment for the habit. All the needs of the sick were given free, in addition to the treatment materials needed for those who did not stay in the hospital. The daily cost was large when added to the salaries of the nurses.

When Dr. Parker gave the work of the hospital over to me, he was able to leave money that would meet only the costs of the current month. Unable to guarantee their pay, his workers left. As my first task, I told the situation to the people of our little church. Some offered to help. Like me, they would depend upon the Lord. Together, we continued to wait upon God. We knew that in some way, He would provide for His own work.

Day by day, the medical store was used up. When it was almost gone, an unusual letter containing a check came to me from a friend in England. The letter said that this person had recently lost his father and he had received his property. Not wishing to increase his own spending, he wanted to use the money to help in the Lord's work. He wrote that I might know of some special need for it, but left me free to use it for my own need or in any other way that the Lord might lead me. He only asked to know how it was used and if there was need for more.

After giving thanks with my beloved wife, I called my helpers into our little worship room and read them the letter. I need not say how happy they were. Together we gave praise to God. They returned to their work in the hospital with full hearts and told the sick people what a God was ours. They asked the people if their gods had ever given them help in this way. Both helpers and the sick received blessing through this remarkable gift. From that time, the Lord gave all that was necessary to continue the work of the hospital, to provide for my own family and the care of other areas of missionary work. Nine months later, I had to give up this work because of my poor health, but I was able to leave more money for the continued work of the hospital than when I began.

But not only was money received in answer to prayer. Many lives were saved from death. People who seemed to be hopelessly diseased were made well. There were good results in cases of serious surgery. There was the case of one poor man whose legs were cut off in a very bad situation. Healing took place so quickly that both wounds were well in less than two weeks.

And greater results than these were received. Many believed in the truth of Christ and called to the Lord in faith and prayer, experiencing the power of the Great Physician[2] to cure the sin-sick soul. During this nine months, sixteen sick people from the hospital were baptised, while more than thirty joined some Christian church in the city.

The year 1860 began with demands for service all sides. But there was not enough time and strength to make full use of the openings we saw. For some time, the shortage of workers had been a serious problem. In January, prayer was made to the Lord of the harvest[3] that He would send out more workers into this special area. On January 16, 1860, I wrote to family at home in England. I told about the deep desire of our hearts like this:

"Do you know any serious young men who desire to serve God in China, who do not want more than their real need and would be willing to come out and labor here? Oh, for four or five such helpers! They would probably begin to preach in Chinese in six months time. In answer to prayer, the necessary means for their needs would be found."

But no one came to help us. With the departure of Dr. Parker, the continued hard work of body and mind and the ongoing effort of other missionary work, my own health began to fail quickly. This caused us to wonder if we needed to return to England for a time.

The thought of returning was hard to face. The growing church and work seemed to need us to be there. It was very difficult to part from those we had learned to love in the Lord. Thirty or forty Christians had come into the recently organised church. The well-filled meetings and the warm hearts of new Christians all looked to a future of much promise. At last, taken down by many attacks of sickness, the only hope of my getting better seemed to be in returning to England for a short stay in its healthier temperature. Though painful at the time, it proved to be only another way for God to show His faithfulness and loving care because He "works out everything in conformity with the purpose of his will."

As before, the Lord was present with His help. We received the means for our trip and enough extra that we were able to bring with us a Chinese Christian to help in translation[4] and to teach the language to new missionaries that the Lord would call for the continued work of the Mission. We knew that He would give us fellow workers. We had been asking Him in careful and believing prayer for many months before.

Before leaving China, we wrote to our friend, Mr. W.T. Berger, whom we had known in England and who had always strengthened our hands in the Lord in that distant land:

"We are bringing with us a young Chinese brother to help us in writing and I hope in teaching the language to those whom the Lord may cause to return with us."

During the voyage, our cry to God was that He would rule over our stay at home for the good of China and make a way to raise up five missionaries to labor in the area of Chekiang. We must tell how the Lord answered these believing prayers and the way in which He honoured them.

[1] Dispensary: a place where medical aid is given.

[2] Physician: doctor. By "Great Physician" is meant God.

[3] Harvest: gathering crops or the season to gather crops.

[4] Translation: to change from one language to another.

CHAPTER EIGHTEEN

# A New Work Needed

"For my thoughts are not your thoughts, neither are your ways my ways," says the Lord. "As the heavens are higher than the earth, so are my ways higher than your ways and my thoughts than your thoughts." How true are these words! When the Lord is bringing in great blessing in the best possible way, how many times our unbelieving hearts are feeling, if not saying, like Jacob of long ago, "Everything is against me!" Or we are filled with fear, as the disciples were when the Lord, walking on the water, came near to quiet the troubled sea, and took them quickly to a safe place.

Yet common sense should tell us that He, whose way is perfect, can make no mistake. He has promised to "perfect (or fulfil) that which concerns" us. In His care He counts the very hairs of our head and forms for us the things that happen to us. He must know better than we, the best way to finish our work and bring glory to His own name.

Blind unbelief is sure to go the wrong way
And see His work as useless;
God has His own design,
And He will make it clear.

It seemed a great loss to me that my health failed, causing me to give up work for God in China just when it had more fruit than ever before. I had to leave the little group of Christians in Ningpo who needed much care and teaching. This was a time of great sorrow. The sense of loss was no less when medical advice told me that it was not possible for me to return to China for years to come. Little did I know then that my long stay in England was a necessary step toward the beginning of work which God would bless as He has done for the China Inland Mission.

In China, there was such great pressure of work that needed to be done around me that I could not think of the much greater need in the areas more inland! Even if I could think of them, there was nothing I could do. While I was kept for some years in England, I saw the whole country on the large map on the wall of my study. In my heart I was as near to the large areas of inland China as to the smaller areas where I had worked for God. Prayer was the only way that the pain of my heart could be helped.

As a long time away from China seemed to be necessary, the next question was how best to serve China while in England. This led to my work for several years with Rev. F.F. Gough of the C.M.S., rewriting the New Testament in the common language of Ningpo for the British and Foreign Bible Society.[G] In doing this work, I saw only the use that the Book and study notes, would be to Christians. But since then, I have often seen that, without those months of studying and feasting on the Word of God, my heart would not have been prepared to begin the China Inland Mission.

In the study of the Holy Word, I learned that to get faithful workers, not to make a great appeal for help, but to pray to God, first to send out workers and then to make the spiritual life of the Church so strong, that men would not be able to stay at home. This was the need. I saw that the plan of the Bible was not to raise great amounts of money. The Bible plan was more to do the work, trusting in His sure Word who has said, "But seek first his kingdom and his righteousness, and all these things will be given to you as well."

In the meantime, the prayer for workers for Chekiang was being answered. The first, Mr. Meadows, sailed for China with his young wife in January, 1862, through the kind help of our friend, Mr. Berger. The second left England in 1864, having her voyage given by the Foreign Evangelisation Society. The third and fourth came to Ningpo on July 24, 1865. A fifth came to Ningpo in September, 1865. The prayer for the five workers was fully answered and our faith was strengthened to look to God for still greater things.

I spent months in prayer about the difficulties involved in the evangelisation of inland China. I was led to know that a special society was needed. I had the daily help of prayer and discussion with my beloved friend and fellow worker, the late Rev. F.F. Gough. Valuable help and advice was also given by Mr. and Mrs. Berger, with whom my beloved wife and I spent many days in prayer. I had the unhappy thought that we may compete with existing missions in England.

By simple trust in God, we decided that a mission might be started and kept going without bringing hurt to any existing effort. I had a growing conviction that God would have me to seek from Him the needed workers and to go back to China with them. But for a long time, unbelief kept me from taking the first step.

How wrong unbelief always is! I had no doubt that God would answer any prayer for workers, "in the name" of the Lord Jesus Christ. I had no doubt that the means for our going out would be given and that doors would be opened before us in unreached areas of the nation. But I had not then learned to trust God for *keeping* power and grace for myself. It was no wonder that I could not trust Him to keep others who might be prepared to go with me. I feared that in the middle of the danger and difficulty, some inexperienced Christians might break down and blame me for having asked them to undertake a great work that they were not equal to.

Yet, what was I to do? Guilty feelings grew stronger and stronger. Simply because I refused to ask for them, the workers did not come forward to go out to China. Every day, several thousand people were dying without Christ. The dying of China so filled my heart and mind that there was no rest day by day and little sleep by night. Finally, my health failed. At the request of my beloved and honoured friend, Mr. George Pearse, I went to spend a few days with him in Brighton.

On Sunday, June 25, 1865, I was unable to stand the sight of a group of a thousand or more people praising God in their own security, while millions were dying for lack of truth. I went out alone in great spiritual pain. There, the Lord gave me victory over my unbelief and I gave myself to God for this service. I told Him that everything must rest with Him and that as His disciple it was my duty to obey and follow Him. His duty was to direct, care for and guide me and those who might labor with me.

Do I need to say that peace came at once into my heart? There and then, I asked Him for twenty-four fellow workers, two for each of the eleven inland areas which were without a missionary, and two for Mongolia. Writing the request on the inside of my Bible, I returned home with peace that I had not enjoyed for months. I had the conviction that the Lord would bless His own work and that I should share in the blessing. I had prayed before and asked others to pray, that workers be sent out to the eleven areas of China that were without missionaries and that their needs be provided for. I had not given myself up to be their leader.

With the help of my beloved wife, I had just written the little book, *China's Spiritual Need and Claims.* Every part of it was clothed in prayer. My friend Mr. Berger had given valuable help in reading the book to check it before it was finished. He paid for printing the 3,000 books. I spoke in every possible place of the work we planned to do. I was especially happy to speak at the Perth and Mildmay Conferences of 1865.

Prayer continued for fellow workers who were soon raised up and invited to my home which was then in the east of London. Our house soon became too small. When our neighbour moved, I was able to rent the house. Later when that was not large enough, more places to stay were provided close by. Soon a number of men and women were under training and involved in missionary work at home. This tested them in many ways as they tried to win souls.

CHAPTER NINETEEN

# The Beginning of the C.I.M.

In the year 1865, the China Inland Mission was organised and the workers in the field became a part of it. Mr. W.T. Berger who was living at Saint Hill, near East Grinstead, took over the direction of the home territory during the time I expected to be away in China. Without his help and good words, I could not have gone forward. As soon as things could be made ready, I would go out and direct the work in the field. For the needs of the workers already in China, our friends at home were giving money we did not ask for. Our every need was being met.

We had now planned for a party of sixteen or seventeen to go out and knew that 1,500 to 2,000 pounds would be needed to cover clothing, passage, and start-up costs. I wrote a little book, calling it *Occasional*[1] *Paper, No. 1*. I planned to write numbered reports to give to donors[2] and friends, informing them of the work done through us in China. In that paper, I told about the needs for starting the work. I expected that God would move the hearts of some of the readers to send money. I had decided never to use a personal request for offerings, to make a collection, or issue collecting-books. A missionary box was permitted and a few were prepared for those who might ask for them. We have continued to use these ever since.

It was February 6, 1866, when I sent my *Occasional Paper, No. 1* to the printer with a design for the cover. On that day, a daily prayer meeting had been begun to ask for the needed money.

On this day we felt much better by having received 170 pounds, 8 shillings, and 3 pence in little more than a month, as we had not asked for such help, except from God. But we also knew that we must ask the Lord to do greater things for us. Otherwise, it would be impossible for a group of from ten to sixteen to leave in the middle of May. Daily prayer was offered to God for the money needed for the clothing and the voyage of as many as He wanted to go out in May.

Because of the delay in printing the Occasional Paper, it was not ready to be to be published until March 12. On this day I looked at my mission money-box and compared the results of the two similar periods of one month and six days each, one before and one after special prayer for 1,500 to 2,000 pounds. It was very interesting. From February 6 to March 12, 1,974 pounds, 5 shillings and 11 pence was received.

"This, it will be seen, was before we sent out the Occasional Paper and was not the result of it. It was the answer of a faithful God to the prayers of those whom He had called to serve Him in spreading the Good News of His Son.

"We can now compare with these two periods of time, a third of the same length. From March 12 to April 18 the money received was 529 pounds. This shows that when God finished providing for the special need, the special income also stopped. Truly there is a living God, and He hears and answers prayer."

But this answer to prayer made it a little difficult to send out Occasional Paper No. 1, as it told of the need which was already taken care of. The difficulty was solved by putting inside each copy, a colored paper saying that the money for the clothing and travel was already in hand in answer to prayer. We were reminded of the difficulty of Moses - not a very common one in this day - and of the message he had to send to the people to bring no more for the building of the Tabernacle.[3] He had to tell them that the gifts in hand were already too much. We believe that if there were fewer requests for money and more dependence upon the power of the Holy Spirit and upon greater spiritual life, the experience of Moses would be a common one in every part of Christian work.

Preparations to sail to China were begun at once. About this time, I was asked to give a talk on China in a village not very far from London. I agreed on the condition that there should be no collection and that this should be written on the announcement papers. The man who invited me said he had never had such a condition requested before. He accepted and the announcements were given for May 2 and 3. With the aid of a large map, something of the population and deep spiritual need of China was presented and many were full of concern.

At the close of the meeting, the chairman said that by my request, there would be no collection. But he felt that many present would be disappointed if they were not able to give something towards the good work. He hoped that as the idea was his own and the feelings surely shared by many in the meeting, I should not object to a collection. I asked that the condition be carried out. I pointed out that among other reasons for having no collection, the very reason given by our kind chairman was, one of the strongest for not having it.

I did not wish for those present to hurriedly give an offering and escape God's dealing with their hearts. This would be easy to do because their hearts felt moved. I asked that each one should go home with a conviction for the deep need for China. They should ask God what He would have them do. If, after thought and prayer, they felt that an offering was what He wanted them to do, it could be given to any missionary society[G] with workers in China. Or it might be given to our London office.

Sometimes God does not want money, but He wants people willing to be in His service in other places. It might involve giving a son or daughter who are more important than silver or gold. I added that I thought the idea of a collection was to give the feeling that the all-important thing was money, but that no amount of money could save one soul. What was needed was that men and women filled with the Holy Spirit should be willing to do the work. For this, there would never be a lack of money. As my wish was seen to be very strong, the chairman kindly accepted and closed the meeting. As we ate supper, he said that he thought it was a mistake on my part. Even with all I had said, a few people had put a little money into his hands.

Next morning at breakfast, my kind friend came in a little late and said he did not have a very good night. After breakfast, he invited me to his study and presented the money passed to him the night before. He told me that he had thought that I was wrong about a collection. He now knew that I was very right. He said that, during the night, he had thought of people in China ever passing into the dark without God. He could only cry as he thought of what I said, "Lord, what will You have me to do?" He said he now had the guidance he asked of God, and here it was. He gave me a check for 500 pounds and said that if there had been a collection, he would have given a few pounds to it. Now, this check was the result of having spent a large part of the night in prayer.

I do not need to say how surprised and thankful I was for this gift. I had received at breakfast a letter from Killick, Martin & Co., a shipping company, in which they said that they could offer us the whole passenger space of the ship *Lammermuir*. I went directly to the ship, found that it was good for our need in every way and paid the necessary amount. As I said before, the money that was needed had been already in hand for some time. But the offer of the ship and this wonderful gift of money was a great help to my heart.

On May 26 we sailed for China in the *Lammermuir*, a party of sixteen missionaries out of twenty-two passengers. Mr. Berger took charge of the home office and so, the China Inland Mission was fully begun.

[1] Occasion: a certain time or at certain times.
[2] Donor: a person who gives (money) for a need.
[3] Tabernacle: the meeting place in the Old Testament.

# ADDITION

By David Bentley-Taylor

When the *Lammermuir* party arrived in China in 1866, they faced the difficult task of bringing the Gospel to the mainland of the country. But they brought to it the weapon of faith and prayer and from their base at Hangchow and Ningpo, the mission work slowly grew out into the territory of Chekiang. As the new workers received experience, they moved out into Kiangsu, Anhwei, and Kiangsi. This took about ten years, during which they suffered much from sickness, death and the lawless people who were fighting against them in their work. Many times they chased them from the cities in which they were trying to settle and preach the Gospel.

Beyond them, the greater part of inland China was still without a Protestant[1] witness for Christ and it was not until 1876 that God, having brought to them many more people, fully opened the way into the main part of China. Then, in two remarkable years, they were able to go southwest to the Burma border, northwest to Mongolia and central Asia, and deep into Tibetan land. When the huge population of China and the great land size of the country are considered, it is clear to see that no work of this size has been done before or since in the history of modern mission work. This work was done through much prayer and sacrifice, not only on the part of the missionaries on the field, but also from friends in their home country.

This first work, from 1878 to 1900 was to go in to explore the area where the China Inland Mission was called to preach the Good News of Christ. This was followed by a period of reaching out and growing a strong church. During this time, the Mission grew until it had many hundreds of men and women who came from Great Britain, North America, Australia, Scandinavia, Germany, Switzerland, and other countries. These were all united under the general direction of Mr. Hudson Taylor, agreeing to put aside minor things they did not agree on and place their concern on their common belief in the Lord Jesus Christ and the main truth of the Gospel as given to us in the Scriptures.

Their work was to win the unsaved for Christ and to build them up into a living church that would honour His name. In these early years of the Mission, results that could be seen were not large. Many of those who turned to Christ were simple country people of little learning. The missionary was not popular and was not always trusted. The more educated Chinese did not like the missionary. He was usually the leader of the Christian group in the area where he lived; he was the center of everything that went on, and most of the money was given by the missionary.

In 1900, this new church and growing mission were called to pass through the great test of the Boxer[2] violence. In three summer months, the C.I.M. alone lost fifty-six missionaries and twenty-three children who were killed, together with hundreds of Chinese Christians. Many other people who were part of the Mission went through extreme difficulty as they tried to reach places where they would be safe.

Looking back, this great sacrifice of life and health was the beginning of a new turn in the story of the work of God in inland China and marked the end of the first part of the history of the Mission. This time was followed by a period of ten years when the missionary, usually seen as the person who came from western culture, was very popular. Many people wanted to be a part of Mr. Taylor's work for reasons that were not good, but such a situation also provided different ways to help. During this time, every part of the work grew.

It was in these days when so many were accepting the Gospel that Hudson Taylor died at Changsha in the heart of inland China. A beautiful end came to a life of Christ-like love and undefeated witness. Few people have ever been so used by God. Few missionaries have seen their prayers so answered and their heart's desire so largely filled.

The work he had left was put through more severe testing when the Chinese War of 1911 took away the secure feeling that was known in the first ten years and brought in a long period of war among the people. During terrible conditions of lawlessness and people being killed, the work of the Church of Christ and the giving out the Gospel continued with more fruit, especially among some of the earliest tribes of China, who turned to Christ in large numbers.

The international work of the Mission made it through the difficulty of the first World War, but conditions in China grew even worse after its close. From 1920 and on, atheism[3] and war continued. In the years 1926-27, it became necessary for a third time for most missionaries to seek safe places on the coast. As at other times, it was not long before they were back inland again. Once more, difficulty and trials turned out to help spread the Gospel. From 1927, it became a goal of the Mission for leadership in every church to be passed from the missionary to the Chinese Christians.

It is easy now to see that without this period of change, a strong national church could never have arisen. In time, foreign money came to be little used except for the care of foreign workers, while the main responsibility in the work and the direction of each church was done by Chinese Christians to whom God had given spiritual gifts. During this period when missionaries were moving out of places of leadership in the local church, the C.I.M. called for many more men and women to bring the Gospel to the millions of people who still lived far beyond its sound. As a result, two hundred new workers sailed from the homeland during 1929-30 and the number of Mission workers rose to its highest number of 1,387 in 1936.

Just when it seemed that under the strong government, a time of greater security was about to start, the conflict with Japan began. Before long, the China Inland Mission was divided into two groups of people living in areas occupied by the army of Japan and the rest in so-called "free China." All the first group were held in a prison after the attack on Pearl Harbor at the close of 1941 and they were not freed until 1945. The Mission workers in the West had to move back before the Japanese army that was going forward.

At one time, the number of active missionaries was down to about 250. Yet these years of great difficulty were rich in blessing. Bible schools for the training of Chinese Christian leaders began to increase during and immediately after the war. A remarkable work of God in the schools of higher learning brought hundreds of students to faith in Christ and began to increase the number of Chinese pastors with a new kind of leadership. When the whole land was open again in 1945 it was found that almost every church that had been cut off for so long, had grown and done much better than before.

But it was only after 1945 that the greatest fruit gathering time of all began. Missionaries who were kept from going because of the war or were just let out of prison, poured back into China to become involved in the on-going work. The trials of the past seemed to have broken up the soul of China and made its ground well prepared for the message of salvation through Jesus Christ.

The things for which Hudson Taylor and the early workers had worked and prayed for were now given in a large way to those workers who came after them. In some places, big meetings became a part of the work and large numbers of people were saved from all levels of society.[G] The future of the church seemed to have no limit, until war broke out, again. In the autumn of 1948, the land began to pass under the control of communists.[4]

This huge change in government brought in a new situation. Government officials who were willing to accept or even think well of missionaries and Christian work were controlled by those whose outlook on life was based on atheism. They took everything that belonged to others and were hostile to any influence that came from the West. Large meetings became impossible, while terrible action against Christians grew. Christians were thought of as being against the government and foreigners were limited in their movements.

New missionaries were unable to enter the country, and the number of missionaries in China was quickly reduced. No man can measure the result of these things or see what future the Lord had for the work which He caused Hudson Taylor to bring into being. But it is good to see that all the great trials and what seemed to be trouble of the past have proved now to be steps to greater blessings.

It is certain that this work to which God called His worker in 1865 has been the means by which a very large number of Chinese have found salvation and hundreds of Christian churches have come into being where at one time the name of Christ was not known. To God be all the glory. Whatever may be the official thinking about foreign missionaries, the Gospel has taken such deep root in China that the witness of Chinese Christians will no doubt continue.

A life like Hudson Taylor's, leading to such wide results, should be looked at very closely. Dr. and Mrs. Howard Taylor have written a two-part history that is a good story both of Hudson Taylor himself and of the happenings of the Mission up to his death in 1905.

To this the book, *Hudson Taylor,* forms a perfect beginning and we invite you to enjoy the fuller record of these great things and to share by prayer, the command of the Lord Jesus Christ to preach the Gospel to every person. The power of prayer cannot be made smaller by distance. Prayer has no limit by age, weakness or daily duty. Changes in the government cannot change its power, for the word still stands, "You may ask me for anything in my name and I will do it." The power of prayer in the life of an obedient Christian can only be done away with by a lack of prayer.

Over one of the doors to the China Inland Mission buildings in London stands the words so close to the heart of Hudson Taylor, "Have faith in God." On either side of it, written in Chinese letters are the two Scriptures which he first proved true in his early days as a missionary, "Thus far has the LORD helped us." and "The Lord will provide." In this spirit we look back and in faith, we face the future.

[1] Protestant: a Christian, one not of the Catholic church.

[2] Boxer: a secret organization that tried to get foreigners and Christians out of China.

[3] Atheism: belief that there is no God.

[4] Communist: one who supports a way of government based on the people owning everything together and no one owning anything alone.

# Glossary

**Apostle:** one sent to do a work, like the twelve disciples of Christ
**Bandage:** the covering put on a wound
**Buddha:** the god of a heathen eastern religion
**Cabin:** a small house or room
**Canal:** like a river, but built by men
**Cannon:** a very large gun
**Captain:** a chief, leader or master of a ship
**Compound:** *1.* to mix or put together *2.* a walled or closed-in area
**Confucianism:** a heathen eastern religion
**Debt:** to owe money to others
**Deck:** floor of a ship
**Diary:** a personal notebook
**Dollar:** the name of money used by several countries
**English money** used in this book:
  Pence or Penny: coin of smallest value
  Shilling: 12 pence
  Florin: 2 shillings
  Half-a-Crown: 2.5 shillings
  Crown: 5 shillings
  Pound or Sovereign: 20 shillings
**Equator:** the unseen line around the middle of the earth
**Hansom:** a hire car pulled by a horse
**Idol:** an object to worship, a false god
**Inland:** away from the sea
**Kingdom:** the country of a king, used here as the place where God's will is done
**Lodging house:** a very low class hotel
**Mandarin:** a high official of China
**Opium:** a drug that is often misused
**Pound:** *1.* a measure of weight, one pound = .454 kg. *2.* name of English money (see *English Money* above)
**Salary:** money received for working
**Sedan:** a chair with long sticks to be carried by two men

**Smuggler:** one who brings in or takes things out, illegally
**Society:** an organised group working together because of a common belief
**Surgeon:** a doctor who operates or does surgery
**Taxi:** hire car
**Teashop:** a place where tea is served
**Thief:** a person who steals in a secret way
**Wheelbarrow:** a box-like tool with one wheel and two handles, for moving small loads
**Yuan:** the money of China

# Note About Special English

Special English is a group of about 1,500 root or basic English words. A different beginning (prefix) and ending (suffix) may be added to these words to change or add to the meaning. For example, when the prefix "un" is added to the word "happy" it becomes "unhappy," meaning "not happy." When the suffix "ly" is added to the word "God" it becomes "Godly," meaning "God like." When these are learned, many more words are easy to understand. Below, is a list of many prefixes and suffixes with their meanings that are used in this book.

**Prefixes:**

dis-: apart, away, not *[disappear, dislike]*
in-: **1.** in, into *[inside]* **2.** not *[indirect]*
pre-: before *[preheat]*
re-: **1.** back *[repay]* **2.** again *[retell]*
un-: not *[untie]*

**Suffixes:**

-able: able to *[readable]*
-ed: **1.** past tense (happened before) *[added]* **2.** having, *[watered]*
-en: **1.** to become, *[weaken]* **2.** made of, *[wooden]* **3.**completed action, *[written]*
-ence: in a condition, or act of, *[silence]*
-er: **1.** one who, *[reader]* **2.** comparing, *[harder]*
-est: more than all others, *[hardest, softest]*
-ful: **1.** full of, like, *[thankful]*
-ing: the act of, *[praying]*; produced by the action of, *[drawing]*; or something that does the action of, *[covering]*
-ion or
-tion: the condition of or result of, *[connection]*
-ive: belonging to or tending to, *[effective, active]*
-less: without *[Godless]*
-ly: like *[Godly]*
-ment: the condition or act of, *[agreement]*
-ness: condition of being, *[greatness]*
-s: plural (more than one), *[Bibles]*